D0390735

THE PRINCETON REVIEW

Speak Smart

THE PRINCETON REVIEW

Speak Smart

BY THOMAS K. MIRA

Random House, Inc.
New York 1998
http://www.randomhouse.com

Princeton Review Publishing, L.L.C.
2315 Broadway
New York, NY 10024
e-mail: info@review.com

Previously published as *Speak Now or Forever Fall to Pieces.*

ISBN 0-679-77868-3

Designer: Illeny Maaza
Illustrator: John Bergdahl

Manufactured in the United States of America on partially recycled paper.

9 8 7 6 5 4

First Edition

DEDICATION

This book is dedicated to Patti, Mike, and Nicole

ACKNOWLEDGMENTS

No book is the work of a single person. This one was the result of a lot of years of learning from a whole group of people who did not even realize they were teaching me. They were my students and clients. Every program, seminar, or problem I have worked on has taught me invaluable lessons that I have tried to include in the following pages.

Thanks to John Katzman and the crew at The Princeton Review, especially Lee Elliott, Alicia Ernst, Kristin Fayne-Mulroy, Meher Khambata, Illeny Maaza, Maria Russo, and Chris Thomas. Special thanks to John Bergdahl for the illustrations.

Thanks to Carol Beekman for helping with the research. Thanks to the Young Presidents' Organization for helping me to strive to be the very best I can be. Thanks to Ken Blanchard, Harvey McKay, Walter Cronkite, Bob Hood, Bob Elliott, Fred Chaney, Doug Glant, Michael Ledeen, Dr. Paul Pearsall, my family, especially my brother Judge Larry Mira, and all my other friends and mentors.

Finally, thanks to Patti, Mike, Coli, and our little pooch Molly. They truly are the joy of my life and the real reason I try.

CONTENTS

Introduction

It's always fun to sit around with friends and shoot the breeze. Nobody cares what the subject is, or who's talking about it—everyone's just hanging out together. Each person discusses whatever grabs him. Some talk incessantly about themselves. Others mention a great movie they saw, or a concert they attended. Still others focus on the latest gossip.

The next time you find yourself in one of these bull sessions, pay attention to how people communicate *just for the fun of it*. I find it fascinating how beautifully people present their ideas when they're not thinking about it. They choose their words instinctively to be understood by the others in the room. They pronounce and articulate the language clearly and understandably. If something isn't understood, the people listening will say "Huh?" and the talker will rephrase. You can hear the emotion in the voice, and see the intensity of feeling in the face and eyes. The hands gracefully complement the story with gestures and subtle nuances, while the body moves and shifts in cadence with the rhythm of the story. The message is communicated, the tale is told, the impact made. Everyone's satisfied and ready to give a response.

The most interesting thing about this type of communication is that it's all done *automatically*. No one is thinking about all these things taking place. They just happen naturally.

But it's also amazing to me how easily these natural communication skills are forgotten in the more pressurized situations we must face from time to time—situations like giving a speech, meeting a new group, presenting a report at a meeting, or briefing an organization about an important issue. These aren't comfortable environments and they cause many people an awful lot of anxiety. In today's competitive world, that anxiety can really mess things up. It can cause us to misstate our message (or completely forget what it was!), which can lead to confusion and misunderstanding. This, of course, plays right into the hands of those who oppose us and are waiting to take advantage of the situation.

Chances are you've read or heard that public speaking is one of our greatest fears. In fact, a number of surveys have shown that many people fear giving a speech more than they do death. If this is true, then it follows that at most funerals, the person giving the eulogy would rather be in the box!

Speaking in public is often the perfect setting for breakdown, but it really doesn't have to be. This book will help you feel confident when the time comes for you to do some public speaking. We'll show you how not to choke. We'll alert you to all the pitfalls of public speaking and help you conquer the fear the whole process can cause. We'll also run through the basic principles of communicating well.

By understanding the levels on which communication takes place, you can develop your ability to make a positive impact on an audience and make it difficult for your opponents to challenge you. Most importantly, you will begin to enjoy, rather than dread, your public speaking engagements. As you proceed through this book, I hope you'll discover the freedom to experience the joy of communicating honestly, openly, and courageously. If you can get yourself "cooking" on the inside—interested in your subject and excited about the chance to tell others—the wonderful and *natural* communication skills we all possess will show themselves on the outside.

CHAPTER 1

Communication: What We Say and How We Say It

Communicating with an audience is the name of the game for any speaker. Let's start out by looking at the four levels of communication.

THE INTELLECTUAL LEVEL OF COMMUNICATION

The first level of communication is the intellectual level—*what* we are saying. If your audience doesn't understand what you are saying, you're not communicating. Everybody already knows this, right? So why is it that so many people have such difficulty being understood? There are three basic ways in which a lack of understanding, or worse, *misunderstanding* occurs.

The first way is very obvious and strangely common:

The audience can't hear you.

Have you ever been to a presentation where the speaker begins in a voice so quiet that no one can make out what he's saying? I have, and what usually happens is that someone in the audience yells out something like "We can't hear you!" This generally causes the speaker to overcompensate by either swallowing the microphone or screaming at the audience. Then, in a very short time, the speaker forgets about the volume problem and returns to his inaudible level. This causes the audience to collectively give up on the presentation. They think to themselves that immortal refrain of corporate America, "The hell with this, I'll wait for the handout!"

When the handout material finally arrives, we take it back to our homes and offices and put it on the pile of "the things I need to get around to reading one of these days." Things that for some reason *never* get read. To help you avoid this problem in your presentations, let me suggest a rule of thumb for volume. It is also the first of the numbered "pointers" you'll find throughout this book (and listed all together on page 159). These pointers are meant to help you quickly reference important points after you've read the book and are getting ready to actually *do* something, like make a speech!

#1 👉 **Find the farthest object in the room and project your voice to that object.**

You will note, I did not say "scream," "holler," "yell," or "bellow" at the object. I said "project" your voice. There's a big difference. Projecting your voice is simply raising it to a level high enough to be heard without losing your natural vocal tone. There are few subtle nuances in a scream, holler, yell, or bellow. You are not calling hogs; you're simply trying to be heard. I've included some breathing exercises at the end of the book that will help you improve both the quality of your voice and your ability to project it.

If the audience is so big that you can't be heard without a microphone, then by all means use one. But never *rely* on the microphone to carry your voice.

#2 👉 **A quiet voice amplified will put an audience to sleep just as fast as a quiet voice unamplified will.**

Many people believe that if they're using a microphone they don't need to project their voices. In fact, they will actually *reduce* their volume to accommodate the microphone. Don't do this. You still need to project your voice, even when you're using a microphone.

Get to the meeting early and test the microphone. By the way, when you test a microphone, don't do dumb things to it. Don't start blowing on it. This is called "spitting on the microphone." And don't start tapping on it, either. This is called "smacking the crap out of the microphone." You also shouldn't get really close to the thing and ask in a quiet voice: "Is it on" or "Can you hear me?" If you do this, the sound technician will turn up the volume. Then, when you begin your presentation in your normal speaking voice, you'll cause everyone's hair to stand on end.

When you're testing the microphone, use the same vocal projection you'll use during the real presentation. If the mike is on a "gooseneck," which is simply a flexible conduit, just bend it toward your face and point it at your *chin*. (Don't point it at your lips because it will pick up all kinds of extraneous noises, like "popping p's" and "sibilant s's," which are really distracting.) Then, count up to ten, then down from ten to one. This will give you a good idea of sound level and will be one less thing for you to stress about. Let the technician, if there is one, adjust the volume of the sound system to accommodate you.

There is another reason for projecting your voice during a presentation, particularly at the beginning: increasing your volume actually reduces anxiety. You are, in effect, converting all that pent-up nervous energy into the physical activity of producing a voice. It helps you focus on what you're doing—not on the fact that you're doing it.

I came to understand this very important idea in a slightly different context.

When I was a kid I used to love to play baseball. I still love the game and even had the great pleasure of coaching my son, Mike, when he was in Little League.

When I was in high school, we had an infamous coach who was absolutely merciless to players who made errors, struck out, or were having bad hair days. You know the type: lots of physical and mental intimidation games. We all have our pet names for people like this.

I can vividly remember going to the plate and looking out at the pitcher and then over to "Coach," who stood at third base with his hands on his hips and a look on his face that said "I know you're gonna blow it, kid, and when you do I'm gonna make you wish you'd never seen a baseball." I started thinking: "Please don't let me screw up. I don't want to put up with all that grief from 'Coach.' He's gonna get right in my face and tell me how worthless I am and I don't need this." About this time a fastball blasted by without my even noticing it. "Strike One!!" the umpire bellowed.

Then I looked out at the pitcher, who was smiling at me, and I thought to myself: "You're not gonna do that to me this time, you #$%*! Throw me something, anything, and I'll put it right over the fence!" He then threw a curveball high and outside, and I swung at it with all of my might...and missed! Strike Two! You can see why I never made it as a big league ballplayer. But I did learn something.

What was the difference between the first pitch and the second pitch? Well, for the first pitch I was totally focused on the fact that I was at bat, in front of a whole bunch of people who were watching me intently. I knew that there was a chance I could fail and that there were severe consequences if I did. I was afraid of screwing up, and *that* was what I was thinking about. With all this racing through my mind, I was lucky I wasn't looking at the umpire and catcher instead of the pitcher! No wonder I didn't see that fastball.

But, for the second pitch, I was just trying to hit the ball! I forgot about all the other things and just tried to hit the baseball. Whether I did in fact hit it or not is irrelevant. There were lots of times when I did. (In fact, I hit the next pitch into center field for a single. The pitcher wasn't smiling at me any more. Neither was "Coach.") Those successes only happened when I stopped worrying about the fact that I was doing something and started focusing on doing it!

Consider this when you face an audience, friendly or unfriendly. Focus on being of real value to your audience. Focus on helping them understand your point of view. Focus on being respectful of them and their worth as human beings.

#3 Focus on what you have to say—not on the fact that you are saying it!

The simple act of increasing your volume will help you reduce your anxiety because it will help you focus on the right things.

The second way miscommunication occurs is also a common one:

The audience can't understand you.

Some people like to impress themselves, or believe they're impressing others, by using hundred-dollar words in their presentations or discussions. I'm sure you've run into these people. They'll start a meeting with comments like:

"Good morning, ladies and gentleman. We are here today to discuss a plethora of problems; a veritable cacophony of concerns that have a spectrum of potentialities that range from problematic to catastrophic and will greatly exacerbate our current dilemma."

I love people like this. They give me a chance to think about what I'll be doing over the weekend, or to put the rest of my day in order and have some time to just relax. No one in the room, including the speaker, knows what she is talking about. But everyone looks attentive and thoughtful. What an unbelievable waste of time!

#4 ☞ **Using conversational language is the best way to assure common understanding among the members of your audience.**

This is particularly true when you are speaking through a translator. In today's rich multicultural soup, this will become increasingly common. If you are using convoluted or difficult language, you face a twofold danger:

1. The translator may not understand the meaning of what you're saying.

2. There may not be a word in the receiving language that approximates the meaning of the word you're using.

Don't take chances with your audiences. Misunderstanding, or lack of understanding, can create opportunities for others to put their own "spin" on what you've said.

Most people understand that straightforward, simple language is the best way to communicate. But there are a few ways language problems can sneak up on you even when you're doing you're best to be clear and understandable. They fall into three categories: jargon, acronyms, and slang. Watch out for these potential communication killers.

JARGON

Jargon is the name given to words or phrases that are specific to a particular industry, technology, or area of study. People who use these words or phrases all the time become so accustomed to them that they begin to assume that everyone knows what they mean. In presentations or discussions they will use this jargon and either confuse their audience or lose them altogether. Listeners are often hesitant to ask for the meaning of the jargon because they don't want to look stupid. The opportunity for meaningful communication has been missed.

To avoid this situation, and for that matter to head off any kind of jargon-related misunderstanding, remember this:

#5 ☞ **If you use a piece of jargon, follow it with a comma and a phrase that explains it.**

Never lose sight of the fact that you aren't giving presentations or holding meetings for your own aggrandizement. You're trying to be of value to the other people in the room. Therefore, it's critically important to present your information in a way that is *understandable* to everyone in the room. So, when you're getting ready for a meeting or presentation, try to set up an "alarm system." If you have the slightest feeling in your gut that someone in the room might either not understand or misunderstand your use of a piece of jargon, then remember to explain the meaning of it. By the way, this is the policy of every major news organization in the world.

ACRONYMS

Acronyms are simply letters that refer to words. For example NAFTA, which stands for North American Free Trade Agreement, is an acronym. Treat acronyms the same way you treat jargon—don't assume the audience knows what an acronym stands for.

#6 The first time you use an acronym, give its full name.

If you use the same acronym later in the discussion, you may want to reiterate its meaning just to make sure everybody understands it. Remember, acronyms were invented to speed up communication. Like jargon, they're meant to act as a sort of verbal shorthand. Used properly they can be very effective. Used excessively, with little or no explanation, they can really confound an audience.

I once met a guy from one of the big aerospace outfits who was wearing a security badge that had the word FNRTNK on it. I asked him what a "fanertnik" was and he said: "Oh, that's an acronym for the project I'm running."

I said: "Yeah, but what does it mean?"

He said: "I just told you that."

I said, exasperated: "No, no. What do the letters refer to?"

He said: "Oh, I'm sorry, I didn't understand what you wanted to know. It's a good question, and many people ask me it."

I started thinking, "This guy is stalling." So I said: "So what do the letters mean?"

An expression of defeat crossed his face and he said: "I forgot. I used to know, but I forgot."

Remember, this guy ran the project!

So watch out for acronyms. They can really screw up a good presentation.

By the way, I never did find out what a fanertnik was. But I'll bet it was expensive.

SLANG

Probably one of the most common ways to confuse an audience is through the inappropriate use of slang. Slang refers to colloquialisms or local usage—words or phrases we use every day that are part of a regional pattern of speech, a cultural expression, or simply the latest cool language. For those who aren't aware of the meaning of these words or phrases, slang can present a terrible communication barrier. In some settings it can even make members of the audience feel excluded from the "in" group. This can result in embarrassment and hostility.

I remember a serious slang problem I created for myself at a tender age. My family lived in the New York City area for the first fourteen years of my life. We then moved to Santa Monica, California. When I was a kid growing up in New York we used certain slang words to describe things. The one I used most often was "*wicked.*" "Wicked" described anything that was special. A beautiful day was a "wicked" day. A particularly attractive car was a "wicked" car. You get the idea.

Well, when we moved to Santa Monica, I had to become acclimated to a very different culture. Everything that was "wicked" in New York was "bitchin" in California. I was happy to meet my new friends and quickly got caught up in the new way of communicating. After all, I was fourteen and had to get accepted as quickly as possible.

Pretty soon everything was "bitchin." It was a "bitchin" day, a "bitchin" car, and a "bitchin" surfboard. "Bitchin" had become a major part of my vocabulary.

One evening, I was having dinner with my Sicilian father, my Irish mother, my even more Irish grandmother, my older sister, and my two older brothers. Dinner was progressing just fine until my mom asked a question of no one in particular. She simply said: "How's the chicken?" I immediately blurted out an answer: "Bitchin, Mom!"

I might have been fine if I had just said "Bitchin!" I should have said "great" or "delicious" or even "wicked." But, I didn't. I said "Bitchin, *Mom!*" My dad heard the first part of the first word and all of the second. The next thing I knew his face was within a fraction of an inch of mine, and he was reaching for his belt and asking me how I dared talk to my mother that way. I tried to explain that I hadn't said anything wrong. I told him that I had said bitch-*in*. His face clouded with confusion for a second. He decided to be fair. He asked my oldest brother Tony (who is eight years older than I): "Anthony, what does this word mean?" My brother smiled benevolently at his wretched little "baby of the family, can do no wrong, everybody's favorite" brother and said: "Kick his butt, Dad, it's worse than you think."

It wasn't pretty.

#7 👉 Be very careful about the use of slang in your presentations. Be sure everyone will understand what you mean.

The third way a lack of understanding or misunderstanding can easily occur also happens a lot:

The audience can't make out the words you're saying.

Be very careful about the *pronunciation* and the *enunciation* of the words you're using. Let's look at these two things.

First, it's very important to pronounce the words you're using properly. If you don't, you're likely to create confusion. Pronouncing words properly is simply obeying two old rules: put the right emphasis on the right syllable, and watch out for tricky vowel sounds.

Now this seems like a relatively simple idea, and it is. But you have to be alert, particularly with technical terms. For instance, do we give a *pre*zentation or a *pree*zentation? Is it fin ANCE or FInance? If you're not sure, look up the word in the dictionary and determine the correct pronunciation.

I was once conducting a presentation technique seminar for a large East Coast company. The president was a tough individual who did not like to be critiqued. He visited our class to tell us how important good communication was to the success of the company.

At the time there was a great storm of controversy surrounding deaths from toxic shock syndrome, which is associated with the use of tampons. The president wanted to use this story to help make some point. He said: "The controversy over *tampoons* is a good example of what I am driving at!"

Everybody in the room looked at each other with the question "Did he just say *tampoons*?" in every expression. Soon smiles began to appear on faces and muffled laughter could be heard. Then the president said it again, confirming our worst suspicions. Apparently, he believed that the way you were supposed to pronounce the word "tampon" was *tampoon*! For the remainder of the presentation the president was bewildered as to what everyone was smiling about. It was not a good way to communicate his seriousness about the points he was making.

#8 👉 Be sure to pronounce words correctly. If you are not sure about a pronunciation, look the word up in the dictionary.

But, even if you are pronouncing words correctly, a much more common and insidious cause of misunderstanding is still lurking. How are you *enunciating* the language? Are you clearly *articulating* the words? In a lengthy presentation, this can be a major problem.

If you're going to give speeches and other presentations with energy and enthusiasm, you're going to get tired. When that happens your entire vocal system becomes less efficient. The diaphragmatic muscles that push the column of air over your vocal chords get tired. This causes your volume to decrease. Many times you won't be aware of the drop.

In addition, your jaw muscles will tire and your mouth will close a bit. So will your tongue muscle, which helps you form your words. As a result, you begin to slur your words. "P's" begin to sound like "T's" and "F's" like "S's." Soon whole words are slopped over and you begin to die the agonizing "death of a thousand cuts," losing members of the audience one or two at a time, as they try to figure out what you just said.

To avoid this fate, be aware of the following:

#9 👉 Concentrate on clear, crisp articulation throughout your presentation.

I know that sounds like an obvious suggestion, and it is. But, here's something to think about. Whenever you're aware of your articulation, it tends to improve. I've had many people in my seminars with varying degrees of nonpathological articulation difficulties. When these problems have been pointed out to them, the improvements have always been significant.

If you feel that you might have a bit of an articulation problem, here's a little exercise that should help:

Read something aloud for three minutes, two or three times a day. While you read it, overarticulate each word. This will do two things to improve your articulation. First, it will improve the efficiency of the jaw and tongue muscles that *help form the words you are saying. You'll develop a better instrument. Second, you'll train your ear to hear yourself articulate cleanly and crisply. In other words, you'll get used to sounding more articulate.*

We have had great results with this simple little exercise. We've seen significant improvement in the first week. In many cases, permanent improvement has occurred in a few months. One note of caution: if you are going to do this exercise at home, let your family or roommates know!

As you can see, the intellectual level of communication is a critical one. So, remember to choose your words carefully and within the level of understanding of your audience. If you're not sure about your audience's understanding of certain words, briefly explain them. Project your voice to the farthest object you can see to be sure you're being heard, to energize the room, and to help reduce your anxiety. Pronounce your words properly and articulate them clearly.

If you do these things, something wonderful will happen: everyone in the room will know what you said. There will be no room for equivocation, no room for debate. Some people may disagree with the *position* you have taken, but they can't credibly deny the clarity of what you've said. You will be understood!

THE EMOTIONAL LEVEL OF COMMUNICATION

Once your audience has heard and understood what you have said, they must *react* to it. This reaction is usually not intellectual. It is *emotional*. Therefore, you'll need to be aware of the second level of communication: the emotional level. An audience's reaction to what you say is based on many variables. Those factors include:

The kind of day each person in the audience is having.

Other things happening to the audience as a whole. Layoffs? Wage disputes? Bad morale?

What's going on at home.

What the audience thinks of your organization.

The nature of their last encounter with you or another member of your organization or industry.

Whatever else the audience has to do *during* your presentation.

These and myriad other considerations shape an audience's response to you. Virtually all of them have an emotional basis. But emotion doesn't stop with the audience. You also need to be aware of the role your own emotions play. First and foremost, you'll need a strong commitment to what you're saying.

There is an old and fundamental premise for good communication:

#10 👉 **You will *get* from an audience exactly what you *give* them.**

I'm sure you know this from your own experience as an audience member. If the speaker is terribly nervous, you become empathetically nervous. If the speaker is enthusiastic, you become enthusiastic. If the speaker is arrogant, his credibility drops significantly.

So, if you want an audience to feel something, you have to feel it first. There are definitely going to be times, particularly during more challenging presentations, when you won't feel very good about your situation. Just remember that if you show your audience that you aren't pleased to be with them, they'll respond accordingly.

> *According to psychiatrist John H. Reitmann, it takes an average person almost twice as long to understand a sentence that uses a negative approach as it does to understand a sentence phrased in a positive way.*

It's terribly important to let an audience know that you care about them, respect them, and are there to be helpful to them. This is particularly true when there are people in the group who, for whatever reason, feel hostile toward you or what you have to say. If the majority of the audience feels friendly toward you it will be much harder for these predators to attack.

There is another reason you'll need to demonstrate an emotional commitment to what you're saying.

#11 👉 **An audience owes you nothing!**

Just because a group of people showed up for your presentation doesn't mean they owe you their attention or their agreement. They may have an interest in the subject, or they may simply have nothing better to do.

On the other hand, I honestly believe that you owe your audience the best presentation of your material you can provide. The audience has given you their time. It is your responsibility to use that time, to the best of your ability, to their advantage.

Therefore, you must be the most interesting thing in the room. If you aren't, the audience will listen to whatever is. It may be the humming of an air conditioner, the gastric rumblings of a person sitting nearby, or, in some cases, snoring.

In other words, you must demonstrate genuine interest in your subject. If you don't appear to believe in what you're saying, why should the audience believe it? If you're not excited about a product, service, or approach to a problem, why should the audience be?

For many technical professionals this is a difficult concept to accept. Technical people are trained with the notion that "the data carry the message." Either a piece of equipment will work or it won't. Either a solution to a problem is correct or it is not. All the yelling, screaming, and wild drum banging in the world won't change the data. So why bother with all this wasted effort?

The answer to that question lies in how audiences make decisions. For the most part, audiences accept or reject arguments based on the believability of the presenter. If we think we can probably trust and believe the speaker, we're much more willing to accept his or her position. Aristotle understood this thousands of years ago. He called it pathos. We call it credibility.

If the speaker isn't committed to the position she has taken, or if it appears that way, the audience will have great difficulty accepting and supporting it. This is true no matter how impressive the data, no matter how accurate the calculations, no matter how technically valid the approach to a problem might be.

My coworkers and I found this out in the early seventies, when nuclear power was being debated. I had just graduated from college and was working for a large electric utility company. I would often accompany our engineers to their public presentations. Invariably, they would go into excruciating (and accurate) detail about the extensive safety precautions that are taken at nuclear power plants. It was usually presented in a very controlled, very technical, totally boring manner. The presenter tended to rely on the data to convince the audience of the safety of the plants. There was virtually no emotional impact to the presentation.

The audience would listen politely to our engineer. Then, someone who was opposed to nuclear power would say something like: "Well, you can believe all that technical gobbledygook if you want to. Just remember, if this guy is wrong your children are going to die horribly from radiation poisoning! Do you want that on your conscience? Well, *do you*?!"

No contest. Game, set, match.

Our engineers had great difficulty understanding how their defeat had come about. They had done everything they were supposed to do. They had studied the issue. They had prepared an accurate and objective review of the problem. They had explained, in careful detail, the solutions to the technical issues. They had even explained the astronomical odds of a problem ever arising. They had done all of this, and still they had been rejected. How could such a thing happen?

It happened because the *emotional* impact of the opponent's position was much stronger than the *intellectual* impact of the engineer. If the engineer had thought more about the concerns of the audience and less about the technical aspects of the issue, the outcome might have been different.

We learned that it is important to establish a personal relationship with the audience. Credibility is not just a matter of technical credentials. It is a matter of personal trust. Our engineers had to share a common bond with the audience—namely, that they were parents, too. The engineers and their families lived in the same area and would be subject to the same risks as anyone else. Furthermore, the engineers needed to tell the audience that they would never, ever place their families in jeopardy.

Finally, the engineers needed to demonstrate their *personal* beliefs in what they were saying. They needed to let the audience know that they had raised the very same questions that the audience had raised. They had studied the issues carefully and reached a reasonable conclusion. At the same time, our engineers had to demonstrate respect for those who disagreed with them. After all, the opponents were entitled to an opinion—the engineers just happened to disagree with them.

This is pretty mushy-headed stuff for a technical professional, but it really does work. It works because it is the proper, respectful thing to do, not because it is an effective technique.

#12 ☞ **It is not just *what* you say that counts— it's *how you say it*. If you mean what you say, say it like you mean it.**

We'll probably never know how many wonderful ideas, inventions, and discoveries have been ignored because of the way they were presented. A poor presentation of a great idea makes an easy target for attack. To make sure that you present your ideas in the best possible way, keep these things in mind:

- **Do not** understate your excellence.

- **Do not** rely on the data alone to convince your audience.

- **Do not** bet your presentation on your graphics.
- **Do** get excited about your presentation.
- **Do** have the courage to demonstrate your enthusiasm.
- **Do** engage your audience and be responsive to them.
- **Do** remember that you are giving the presentation for the benefit of the audience.
- **Do** be respectful to those who may disagree with you.

 If you do the things I've outlined in this chapter, you will be a much better speaker and have a heck of a lot more fun doing presentations.

CHAPTER 2

Nonverbal Communication: How We Say What We Don't Say

Visualize yourself in this situation: you are giving a presentation to a customer group. In the room are about ten people, not including yourself. Sitting at the head of a long conference table is the senior member of the group. She is the decision maker. You begin your presentation and you focus your attention on the boss. After all, she's the one you have to convince, right?

As you proceed, you notice that the boss is paying close attention. She is watching you and occasionally writing down some of the things you are saying. Suddenly, you see her nod her head at you and indicate that you have made a good point.

You think to yourself: "Hot dog! The boss is on my side!"

As you continue your presentation, you say something that seems to bother the person sitting mid-table, a few seats down to the left of the boss. This guy is in clear view of the boss at all times. The person reacts, but does not say anything. You don't notice his reaction because you are so mesmerized by the fact that the boss agrees with you that you can't take your eyes off of her.

You finish your presentation with a flourish and say: "Well, what do you think?" (You secretly giggle to yourself because you already know the answer. You are going to get the deal and you're already planning the celebration!)

In a split second the boss glances over at our friend at mid-table. He looks back at her and gives a single, slight shake of the head. She looks back at you and says:

"We really appreciate your coming to visit us this morning. We will take what you have to say under consideration and someone will get back to you. Thank you so much for joining us.

"Now, what's next on the agenda?"

In complete shock you wonder: "What the heck happened!?"

Here's what happened:

> *You blew it!*
>
> *You missed the opportunity!*
>
> *They're not going to ever call you back!*
>
> *They just kissed you off!*
>
> *You snatched defeat from the jaws of victory!*

How could this have happened? Everything seemed to be going fine! What went wrong?

Here's what went wrong:

You weren't watching what was going on in the room so you missed the nonverbal dialogue.

READING BODY LANGUAGE

If you talk to any behavioralist, he will tell you that about 80 percent of human communication is nonverbal. This is a very important point. It can make the difference between a successful presentation and a failure like the one we just saw.

Many people feel that when they're giving a presentation they have the responsibility to move around, smile, twinkle their eyes, and gesture in order to hold the audience's attention. They're right, but that's only part of the responsibility. A speaker must also keep her eyes on the audience to see what they are saying *back* during the presentation.

#13 **A presentation is a communication among a group of individuals, one of whom is speaking *aloud* at any given time.**

Think about the last time you gave a presentation. You probably spoke, and the people in the audience asked questions or made some comments. As you were speaking, I'm sure you noticed one or two people nodding their heads in agreement and others just looking back at you. You might even have noticed a few "dozing head snappers." You know what these are. No, they're not a new breed of intelligent, carnivorous fish that hang out at presentations. They're that breed of people who fall asleep during presentations and meetings.

We've all seen this phenomenon. These folks close their eyes, and their heads slowly descend toward their chests. When the head reaches a certain point, usually contact *with* the chest, or when some loud noise occurs in the room, the head snaps back and the eyes fly open. The person then looks around the room sheepishly and pretends to be intensely interested in the discussion for a few moments. Then the whole process begins again.

If a dozing head snapper has ever graced a presentation *you've* given, you no doubt responded in some way. As the nodding began, you spoke more often to the person. You checked the "lookers" to make sure they were still looking and you spoke louder or accidentally on purpose bumped the microphone to wake up the snappers.

In other words, you were having nonverbal dialogues with these people as you went through your presentation. You were telling them what was on your mind and they were giving you feedback as to whether the message was received. Each individual responded differently, but they all responded. You, in turn, responded to them and the process continued.

Or maybe you had a different experience at your last presentation. Did you spend most of your time looking at your notes? Reading your visual aids to the group? Looking at your shoes? Or casting your eyes heavenward for divine intervention? If you were doing these things you missed a big part of your own presentation. That's a shame.

It's not easy to look at an audience. It's much more comfortable to concentrate on other things and avoid the pressure the audience puts on a speaker. However, ignoring the audience is always a big mistake. It's terribly important, particularly in more pressurized environments, to be continually aware of the mood of the audience. It's also important to identify your friends and determine where any potential problems are lurking.

The only way you're going to do this is by looking at the audience. You've probably been told to make eye contact with the audience because it involves them and makes them feel good.

That's a valid and worthwhile suggestion, but it's only part of the reason for keeping your eyes on the audience. The other reason you need to look at your audience is to keep aware of what is happening in the room while you're presenting so you're able to make adjustments.

#14 **Always give your audience eye contact because:**
1. **It involves your audience.**
2. **It keeps you aware of their reactions to what you say.**
3. **It helps you identify friends and predators.**

Let's return now to the scenario we were discussing earlier.

If you had been making good eye contact you would have noticed that the guy at mid-table had a problem with what you were saying. He might have arched an eyebrow, sort of like Mr. Spock. He might have shaken his head or narrowed his eyes. He might have picked up his Mont Blanc and made a note while slightly shaking his head. He might have put his pen down and leaned back in his chair with his arms folded. He might have sighed. He might even have said something. Now, that would have been very helpful. At least you would have had a chance to hear his objection and respond to it. In this case, he chose not to respond verbally. However, he *did* respond.

Let's assume for just a moment that you *had* noticed his reaction. What would you have done? Here are some alternatives:

(A) Ignore it, but file it away for future reference.

(B) Ask the group if they have any questions.

(C) Try to figure out what he reacted to and rediscuss it.

(D) Call on Mr. Mid-table.

All of these alternatives are used by presenters in these sorts of situations. However, in the situation we're discussing there is one best solution. Let's review the options and see how they would work out.

In choice A, you would notice the reaction but choose to ignore it and make a mental note. Unfortunately, you would never get a chance to deal with the concern. Once you'd finished, the boss would have simply looked at Mr. Mid-table, noted his reaction, and dismissed you without discussion. Mr. Mid-table's head shake was good enough for her to make the call. So, waiting to respond would not have been the right move.

Choice B suggests you ask the group if there are any questions. There may indeed have been questions, but they might not have come from Mr. Mid-table. The questions might have led you off into a series of side issues that had nothing to do with his concern. At the end of the presentation, the boss would still look at Mr. Mid-table, who would still shake his head. Result: you lose again.

In choice C you would try to guess what Mr. Mid-table reacted to and deal with it. Unless you have incredible mind-reading capabilities, this approach rarely works. Invariably, when someone tries it he guesses wrong and ends up looking very silly. He rehashes information and appears to be defensive. Meanwhile, Mr. Mid-table's itch has not been scratched and the meeting ends on that same sour note.

I prefer the direct approach, which in this case is choice D. By calling on Mr. Mid-table I can bring his concern to the surface and have an opportunity to deal with it. But I must do this in a way that does not put Mr. M. on the spot, which might anger him and create an enemy.

I once saw one of my clients look at a member of his upper management, an important internal customer, and say:

"You look confused. Can I help?" Now I'm sure my client did not mean to offend his customer. He was just trying to be helpful. However, it's not a smart move to make your customer feel like a moron.

Another time, in a public meeting, a very defensive company representative noticed a member of the audience frowning.

He blurted out: "Do you have a problem?" Again, he was only trying to be helpful. It just came out wrong. The result: if the frowning audience member didn't have a problem before, he sure had one now!

So, you see, it's not just that you have to be able to spot a concern. You must be able to draw it out of the person without embarrassing her. It's very important that the speaker take responsibility for facilitating the communication of information. Consider saying the following to Mr. M.: "Sir, you look concerned about something I said. May I clarify anything for you?"

Notice that I'm placing the responsibility for any misunderstanding on my shoulders, not on Mr. Mid-table's. He now feels free to either tell me what's on his mind or say that everything's fine. This also places me in a very strong position with the boss. She'll see that I'm interested in making sure all issues are discussed, and that I'm concerned that everyone has a clear understanding of my information. I have also made it very difficult for Mr. M. to kill my presentation with a single head shake. If he has had an opportunity to raise concerns, how can he just dismiss my entire presentation without some sort of explanation? The answer is, he can't.

There is another issue here: it may very well be that the nonverbal message that Mr. Mid-table communicated might have been totally unrelated to your discussion. Something he had to do might have popped into his head, and he reacted. Perhaps he left the lights on in his car and it just dawned on him. Perhaps he has to go out to dinner with a particularly obnoxious customer and he just thought of it. By calling on him you will jolt him back to the meeting and give him a chance to say that everything's OK.

The point of all of this is that you will never have the opportunity to deal with these kinds of situations if you're not looking at your audience.

It's also very important to appropriately interpret the information coming to you from your audiences. As we've already seen, nonverbal communication can be tricky. What we see does not always mean what we think it means.

Here's an example: let's assume for a minute that I'm some important person and that you are presenting some important information to a group of which I'm a part. When you start your presentation I'm sitting forward in my chair and leaning on the conference table in front of me. I'm smiling at you, paying attention to what you're saying with close eye contact, and even nodding in places.

As you continue, you notice that I lean back in my chair and fold my arms in front of me. To some, this means that I have closed myself off to the communication. That may very well be the case. But it could also mean that I'm cold, or it could be that I always sit this way when I'm really listening.

You go on and you see me put one finger over my lips without unfolding my arms. To some, the simple act of putting one finger over my lips indicates that I'm evaluating what you're saying and I'm essentially shushing myself. This also could be the case here. But it also might be that my denture adhesive grip is losing its hold and my finger is saving me a rather nasty little moment.

You forge ahead, but now you see me turn in my chair so that I'm sort of looking at you sideways. Finally, you see me cast my eyes to the floor and it dawns on you that you're in deep trouble.

In this case, I gave you a group of nonverbal signals that were providing information. Please notice that I said a *group* of signals. This is an important distinction. Don't react to a single signal. Instead, you should respond to what people in the behavioral sciences call "nonverbal clusters."

#15 👉 When reading nonverbal information look for "clusters" of information, *not* individual signals.

There were two distinct nonverbal clusters in the above scenario.

Nonverbal Cluster 1
When you started your presentation I:

- Sat forward in my chair.
- Leaned on the conference table in front of me.
- Smiled at you.
- Paid attention to what you were saying with close eye contact.
- Nodded at you, giving you positive feedback.

This cluster of nonverbals gave you the information you needed to know that your message was being received and responded to in a positive manner. Each one of these actions in themselves provide a great deal of information. But, together, they send a *very* powerful message to the speaker.

Nonverbal Cluster 2

Similarly, when things started going badly, I was giving you another cluster of nonverbal messages. I:

- Leaned away from you.
- Crossed my arms across my chest.
- Placed a finger over my lips.
- Turned away from you.
- Looked at you out of the corner of my eye.
- Finally, broke all contact with you.

Don't you feel awful?

In this case, the initial signals I sent were inconclusive. As time went by, the additional signals gave you the information you needed to come to the conclusion that I was not thrilled with your message. As this scenario demonstrates, it's very important that you look for nonverbal clusters, *not* single signals.

I recommend that you read some of the many excellent books around that deal with nonverbal communication. A good start is Body Language *and the older but still interesting* Subtext, *both by Julius Fast. Another excellent book is* How to Read a Person Like a Book *by Henry Calero and Gerald Nierenberg. Finally, don't miss Roger Axtell's fascinating and useful book* Gestures, *which discusses how body language differs around the world.*

At this point, you have an idea of what you should be looking for when you're giving a presentation or just participating in a meeting. Now let's talk about what your audience should be looking at.

NONVERBAL TOOLS OF COMMUNICATION

Nonverbal tools make up the rest of the nonverbal communication cycle. In fact, what you do with your face and what you do with your body during your presentation are so important that they make up the third and fourth levels of communication. As we discuss the options you have for using your face and body to communicate, try to think of these options as a pile of tools. We'll discuss how to use each one, but everyone will use them slightly differently. Take the time to experiment and find out which tools are the best for you.

FACIAL EXPRESSIONS

Have you ever been to a presentation and been uncomfortable with the presenter but can't quite pinpoint why? I certainly have. In many cases it's simply because the presenter's facial expression doesn't match what he's saying. But the expression on a speaker's face is crucial to what he communicates. For example, a speaker plans to discuss an important and serious subject. He's nervous about the presentation and concerned about doing a good job. He enters the room and looks at the audience members. They appear as serious as he feels. He begins his presentation with the happy words:

"Good morning, ladies and gentlemen. I am delighted to have the opportunity to present the results of a study conducted by a truly outstanding group of people."

All the while he has the same stricken look on his face that he had when he entered the room. He is saying something that is clearly upbeat, yet his expression is somber.

Meanwhile, across the country, another speaker decides to lighten up a serious presentation with a little humor. She begins her talk with a funny story about her life. She gets a good laugh, and with a great big smile on her face begins the main part of her presentation:

"I am here today to announce a rather significant reduction in force that will take effect immediately."

Understandably, people in the room begin to ask each other what the hell she is smiling about. The expression on the speaker's face does not match what she is saying, and the audience is left confused and annoyed. This scenario repeats itself on a daily basis all over the world. It goes back to the basic problem so many speakers confront, which we discussed in chapter one: they focus on the fact that they are giving a presentation rather than on what they have to say. It's one of the most common and destructive mistakes a speaker can make.

#16 The expression on your face must match the meaning of the words you are using.

If your expression doesn't match your message, it creates a real problem for your audience. They can't tell what you really think. Do you care about what you're saying or not? The audience must feel you do if they are going to believe you. You're sure to be challenged by someone if the expression on your face indicates that even *you* don't buy what you're saying.

Your face actually does two things for you. First, it communicates, and second, it's a big part of your personal trademark.

Quick, think of Ronald Reagan. Don't think about it, just do it.

Now think of Mick Jagger.

Now think of Meryl Streep.

I bet you saw the *face* of each person I asked you to think about. That's because we tend to remember people by their faces. So, it's important that we use our faces to make a good impression on our audiences and leave them with a positive memory after our communication is over.

Your face communicates, *if you will let it.* The problem is that most of us tend to hide our faces when we're communicating. Psychologists call this "masking." In some cases, like poker games and tough negotiation settings, this masking is the right thing to do. Later on, I will show you how you can use your face in an adversarial encounter. To a great extent, that will qualify as masking, too.

But, for now, it's important to remember that when we are trying to communicate honestly and openly our faces should reflect what we are truly feeling. We are not trying to fool our audiences; we are trying to help them understand our message and know that we are telling them the truth. So:

- If you're happy, it's important to smile.
- If you're sad, it's OK to look sad.
- If you're angry, it's fine to look angry.
- If you're frustrated, you should look frustrated.

The interesting thing about your face is that it will communicate something even when you're trying to stop it from communicating—namely, that you are trying to avoid communicating. By the same token, your face will also communicate other information involuntarily. It seems to me that it's just too hard to spend our time in front of people trying to control our facial expressions, unless we have a powerful reason to do so. Even then it can only be done infrequently and briefly.

The best advice I can give you is to simply allow your face to communicate your feelings to your audience. In return, your audiences will appreciate that you are being honest with them and respond positively to you—*even if they disagree with you.*

Your face is also part of your personal trademark. No one, not even an identical twin, looks exactly like you. No one smiles just like you. No one looks mad just like you do.

No one else in the known universe has your exact set of facial expressions. I think this is terrific! It allows each of us to have a very personal impact on the people we encounter. It allows audiences to like us for ourselves, not just for an opinion they share or a position we might hold.

#17 Use your face to communicate what you are honestly feeling and as a part of your personal trademark.

It is my sincere hope that you will have the courage to share yourself with the people with whom you communicate. It's my desire to showcase you, and, through you, showcase your ideas, beliefs, services, or products. In today's society, there is a growing emphasis on showcasing *things.* Things like machines, technologies, or systems appear to be what is important. There is no question that they are important. I just think that the people, the genius *behind* these achievements, are more important.

Remember that things are easy to attack. They don't fight back and predators love easy prey. A good communicator *will* fight back and will use the tools he has to honestly and straightforwardly state a position. If I trust the person telling me about the thing, I am much more likely to believe that the thing will do what it is supposed to do.

I remember when I was in the difficult position of representing nuclear power plants and there was great opposition to them. The moment I always worked toward was when an opponent would say to me:

"You know, Tom, it isn't you. You seem like a pretty reasonable guy. It's those miserable idiots you work for who are so screwed up!"

I knew then that we were going to stop yelling at each other and start communicating about our points of view. I had earned their personal trust, and through that trust I was given the opportunity to express my views and listen to theirs. In subsequent meetings I would often be recognized and described as "one of the good guys."

THE EYES HAVE IT

Shakespeare said it best: "The eyes are the windows to the soul." It is true that our eyes are very powerful communication tools. Here's a story to make the point. A number of years ago, I had the pleasure of meeting and interviewing Burt Reynolds and Charles Nelson Reilley. Burt has an acting school in Florida and, at the time, Charles was the "artist in residence" teaching classes on technique.

I asked Burt this question: "How can you tell a good actor?"

Burt responded: "By his eyes."

I turned to Charles and asked if he agreed.

He said: "Absolutely, Tomasso!" (We were in Italy at the time.)

At this point, I was a bit confused, so I asked Burt to tell me more. He said that, in reality, there are many things that contribute to a good performance. But, for him, one of the most critical signs is what is happening within the actor's eyes.

Burt said: "If I can see intensity in the actor's eyes then I believe that he has really *become* the character he is portraying. If the eyes are dead, then he is just reciting lines, and that is *not* acting."

I observed that this was probably true in movies, where the camera can get very close to the actor. But I didn't think it was as applicable to stage acting, where audiences are much farther away from the actor. Charles, who has had a successful career on Broadway as an actor and director and has won two Tony Awards, quickly straightened me out on this issue. He commented:

"If I can't see it in their eyes in the first row, I won't see it anywhere in the balcony."

Charles and Burt are correct not only for acting, but for communication in general.

When you are giving a presentation, or simply expressing your point of view in a conversation, your eyes will communicate the depth of your belief and the believability of your position. The nice thing about all this is that you do not have to pretend to believe in something, as actors must. You simply have to communicate how you really do feel about something.

Use a comfortable gaze to look at the person with whom you are speaking. If you are speaking with an audience, look at people around the room. Spend enough time with each individual to get a response—a head nod, a smile, a shift in the seat, or a break in eye contact—then move on to someone else. If someone sticks his tongue out at you or makes some nasty gesture, you will want to move to someone else more rapidly. Make a mental note of it, though: this is someone to look out for.

By making eye contact, you will be able to see the audience and those close to you will be able to see your commitment to your position through your eyes.

#18 👉 **Your eyes communicate commitment and belief. Make sure you let your audience see them.**

It's not just your face that you have to be in control of in order to give a good presentation. The rest of your body, your gestures, and your physical involvement in the presentation all count enormously. Things like head movement and body movement communicate to the audience whether you're interested in your material or would rather be at the beach. First, you need to think about your body in a general sense.

POSTURE

Posture is the way we hold ourselves when we're not thinking about it.

Do you remember when you were just a little kid and your mom or dad or some schoolteacher was always telling you to "Sit up straight!" or to "Stop slouching!" You probably responded by sitting or standing up a little bit straighter for a while. Invariably, when you stopped thinking about it you returned to your usual disgraceful self.

In reality, all those people you perceived as "pains" were doing you a great favor. Posture is terribly important in terms of what and how you communicate. It can have a tremendous impact within the first few seconds an audience lays eyes on you.

The initial impression you make on an audience can make or break your presentation. It can make a huge difference in how an audience will treat you if a predator attacks. If you look like you don't particularly care, they will leave you for the person to destroy. If you look like a stiff, unbending jerk, they're likely to help him do it.

Keep in mind the remarkably small amount of time it takes for an impression to be made.

#19 👉 **An audience's initial impression of a speaker is made within the first three seconds of the time the audience sees him.**

This is good news for you. It means that you can *control* an audience's perception of you within the first three seconds of the presentation!

Here is what you're looking for in terms of posture. First of all, stand at your full height. This does not mean that you need to stand at attention in front of the audience like a new military recruit. It does mean that you should use whatever height you have to your advantage. Many times people who are tall almost seem to apologize for their height when they're presenting. They slouch or bend forward, causing them to look uncomfortable and awkward. If you are a tall person, use your height to your advantage. Your tallness adds to your credibility because you are such an impressive physical presence. It will even cause some predators to think twice about attacking.

If, like me, you are not very tall, slouching around and leaning forward are not going to help your presentation. Stand (or sit) up as straight as you comfortably can. It will make you a more impressive presenter no matter how many vertical inches you consume.

But you'll have to do more than just sit up straight if want to make a great first impression. Your entire physical attitude is on display.

POSITIVE PHYSICAL ATTITUDE

Physical attitude is the way you hold yourself when you *are* thinking about it. At the beginning of your presentation you want to show your audience that you are pleased to be with them, sincerely interested in being of value to them, and confident in your ability to present your material. Take on a "dynamic physical attitude" while giving a speech. It's important to look impressive.

Here's a good way to adopt a positive physical attitude:

1. Stand tall, facing directly toward the audience.

2. Put your feet at a comfortable distance apart in order to stabilize yourself.

3. Throw you weight slightly forward onto the balls of your feet. This will "unlock" your knees and give you a much more assertive stance. By the way, you also want to unlock your knees because standing with them locked for a long time can cause you to pass out. Choir directors and drill instructors have always known this. You don't want to discover it the hard way. Women, be sure to wear low heels on the day of your presentation. This will allow you to move your weight forward without pitching yourself into the first row!

If you happen to be standing behind a lectern, you can still adopt this very positive physical attitude by taking a half step back from the lectern. This will allow you to do all the things I've just suggested and still be able to reach (and read) your notes. I think you'll be pleased with the results.

Having a positive physical attitude and good posture can be very valuable in more difficult, uncomfortable environments. Don't make a sheepish entrance and look nervous and defensive onstage. If you walk onstage looking confident and friendly, you make it more difficult for anyone to attack. It may even cause a potential attacker to back off altogether and wait for weaker prey.

These two items, good posture and a positive physical attitude, are important. But be careful—they can both be undone by the way we decorate ourselves.

GROOMING

With so many books and magazines on the market telling us how we should look, it can often be confusing for a lot of us to decide how to put ourselves together in the morning. I've come to the conclusion that the way you decorate yourself should represent your own style and personality. Your grooming should be a part of your personal trademark.

However, there is a very important issue associated with grooming. In fact, our grooming can have a tremendous impact on how we are perceived by audiences. Improper grooming creates a perfect opportunity for those who may oppose us to separate us from our audiences.

#20 Your grooming should be reflective of your audience and should never be extreme.

One of the most difficult hours of television I have ever watched resulted from a bad grooming decision. It happened many years ago on *Donahue*. Two representatives of a utility company were invited on the show to discuss the problem of "energy theft." "Energy theft" refers to the variety of ways people rip off utilities, from actually tapping into power and gas lines to simply skipping out on the bill. It costs everybody a lot of money every year, and the people at the utility thought it would be a good idea to let the country know about the problem.

So far, so good.

The utility decides to send the manager of public relations and a vice president. We never really found out what this person was vice president *of*, but I guess he must have had some relevant responsibility.

The p.r. manager dressed in his normal manner for the program. He looked like just about every middle manager of the day: rumpled. He had on a rumpled gray suit, short-sleeved shirt, stiff, striped tie (I'm pretty sure it was a clip-on), droopy socks, and unpolished wingtips.

But check out the veep. He took a very different approach. He figured he was going on national television and wanted to look his very best. It appeared that he went out and spent a bundle on his "TV outfit." He was wearing what looked like a Brioni suit. This is a handmade, Italian-cut suit, made of extremely expensive material, in most cases silk. He was also wearing a beautiful silk dress shirt, a silk tie, a collar pin, a diamond pinky ring, over-the-calf men's hose, and Gucci shoes. The guy looked great! After all, he was going on national TV, he should look like a million bucks, right?

Wrong.

The first sign of trouble was when the producers made our two friends sit on the edge of the stage with their feet hanging over, instead of in the usual onstage guest chairs. The show begins. Phil Donahue introduces our buddies and says:

"Well, this is not 'get the utility day,' necessarily. But we are concerned about people who can't pay their utility bills and the often coldhearted manner in which they are handled by the utilities.

"To examine this issue today we have two audiences with us. Way up there in the back we have our usual visitors. But, up here in the front rows we have about two hundred people, all of whom are customers of our guests and all of whom have had their electricity turned off for nonpayment!"

The expression that appeared on the faces of our utility executives is one we have all seen in nature films. You know the ones I mean. The wildebeest with the lion on his back, the rat in the boa constrictor's mouth. These are not happy animals. Neither were our two chum(p)s.

In my world, we refer to this expression as the *"Oh Shit Look."* For purposes of decency we will simply refer to it as the "OSL" from now on.

"Jaws" Donahue now moves to the first question from the audience. He calls on a young African-American woman. She rises, and we see that she is wearing a down jacket that is torn, some feathers sticking out of the tears. She has an old woolen cap on her head with a really chewed-up tassel on the top. She is wearing glasses that are taped in the middle to keep them from falling apart. She has her electric bill in one hand and, in the other, a beautiful little girl huddled close to her.

She looks at our vice president, who also happens to be African-American, and says, with no anger, no hatred, only quiet desperation:

"Brother, how much did that suit cost you?"

Jaws had arranged for the cameras to be right on the end of the nose of the vice president. They captured a very interesting response. First, one of the most definitive OSL's I have ever encountered. This changed quickly to an expression of anger. The poor guy was steamed by the question. He looked at the lady in the audience and said:

"Madam, I don't think that is a relevant question."

This caused a huge upheaval in both audiences as boos erupted and our pals were screamed at from all quarters. It was daytime talk TV at its best!

It was all downhill for our cronies. This was particularly upsetting since what I just described happened within the first sixty *seconds* of a sixty-*minute* program!

As you can see, the wrong choice in grooming can have disastrous effects on your communication. It is important to be respectful of the audience with whom you will be communicating. Your grooming should not get in the way of what you have to say. It should be appropriate to the environment you're going to speak in. For example, if you are going to speak to a group of very senior executives at a large corporation, then you should wear your most businesslike attire. For men, the best bet is a clean, pressed suit, a white or striped long-sleeved shirt, a colorful but subdued tie, over-the-calf socks, and nicely shined shoes. It also means a neat hairstyle and clean, clipped fingernails. Women should stick with suits or well-tailored dresses with jackets. Go easy on the jewelry; it can distract audiences. Also, if you have long hair try to keep your hair back from your face, as it, too, can be distracting.

If you are going to a community meeting or are visiting an organization with a much less formal dress code, try to dress in a way that is reflective of the audience. But remember that it is always an *occasion* to be with an audience. You should always dress in a way that reflects how important the occasion is to you. Remember, it is always easier to take a tie or jacket off than it is to find one at the meeting.

It should be clear by now that good posture, a positive physical attitude, and appropriate grooming can have a very powerful impact on the success, or failure, of communication. If you think about these things *before* the meeting and plan accordingly, you can dramatically increase your probability for success.

Now that we have figured out what to do with the trunk of your body, we have to start thinking about what to do with two very important appendages.

HANDS

Your hands may be the most important part of your body to take into account when you're speaking to a group. I've noticed that many people use their hands really well when they're talking with friends, and put them away when they're giving a presentation. Much of this probably has to do with other people telling them that they use their hands too much when they speak. This makes a speaker self-conscious, and doesn't do the presentation one bit of good. To avoid "overusing" her hands, the speaker hides them somewhere.

Don't allow this to happen to you. Your hands are wonderful tools of communication. If you use them when you are communicating for the fun of it, use them in your presentations, too.

#21 👉 If you use your hands in normal conversation, use them in your presentation.

What if you don't like to use your hands a great deal in regular conversation? In that case, don't worry about them during your presentation. Just keep them available for use, should the urge to make a gesture come over you.

When you are giving a "stand-up" presentation, be sure to keep your hands available. I tend to hold my hands in front of me, at right about the solar plexus. This is just below your sternum. I hold my hands so that the tips of the fingers of my right hand are touching the joints of my left hand. This way, if I want to make a gesture I can do it easily, and if I don't my hands are out of the way.

A lot of people get confused about what they can and can't do with their hands during a presentation. The correct answer is:

You can do anything you want with your hands!

If you want to stand with your hands by your side, it's perfectly OK to do so. Just shake yourself out right before you start your presentation. This will loosen your arms up and make you feel more comfortable using your hands.

If you want to hold your hands in front of you in the classic "fig leaf" pose, that's fine, too. Actors are not allowed to do this sort of thing onstage, but we're not talking about making you an actor. We are trying get you to relax when you're in front of a group so your brain will engage. If standing this way helps, go for it.

Just don't make a "hinge" with your hands by holding the thumb of one hand with the other hand. If you do this, you are in danger of getting the urge to make a gesture and having only the remaining fingers of the captured hand move up. In the trade we call this effect the "flashing fig leaf." This gesture is distracting, as it reminds everyone of a cuckoo clock.

You can also put one hand in your pocket if you are so inclined. You can then make gestures with the other hand. Try not to put both hands in your pockets. If you do so you could seriously injure yourself should you suddenly decide to make a gesture.

One other thing: empty your pockets of all noisemakers such as coins, keys, etc. If you're nervous, you will begin to unconsciously rattle them. Rattling things in your pocket is a dead giveaway that you're in trouble.

If your pockets are empty and you have a hand in one of them, *keep it still*. You don't want audience members distracted trying to figure out what you are doing.

The point of all of this is to let you know that you use gestures every day of your life to help other people understand what you're saying. If you can remember this when you are communicating in difficult environments, your gestures are much more likely to be natural and meaningful.

Whatever you do, don't plan gestures! If you do, I promise you will mess up every time. Just let your gestures happen naturally.

If you are standing at a lectern or podium, or are in a meeting where you are seated at a conference table or witness table, place your hands on either side of your script or notes. If you don't have any paperwork in front of you, simply place one hand flat on the table and place the other hand on top of it. The idea is to keep them available when you need them and quiet when you don't.

This is particularly important if you're at a table where the audience can see your hands. When your hands are moving around they betray anxiety. This will give comfort to the predators and may even cause them to pounce on you. Just keep your hands quiet and focus on helping the audience understand what you have to say.

GESTURES

Gestures are another part of public speaking that should be based on your real personality and the way you communicate under normal conditions. A few genuine gestures are much more impressive than several phony ones. Phony gestures result when speakers are told that they don't use their hands enough when they are speaking. To overcome the problem, speakers concentrate on making gestures during their presentations. This is called "acting," not presenting.

This "acting" issue is a pet peeve of mine. You see, my little cottage industry was founded by actors, *failed* actors. These people couldn't make it in the movie business and decided that they could make a buck teaching the rest of us how to communicate. As a result, the focus became the form of the presentation. The great Shakespeare was often invoked. Students were admonished to "Fit the gesture to the word and the word to the gesture!"

What resulted was a whole generation of really lousy actors. Instead of just telling people what was on their minds, these poor people were knocking themselves out trying to give presentations the way they thought presentations were supposed to be done. It was a real shame.

I have seen it happen many times: the speaker will become so focused on the form of the presentation that he'll lose a great deal of the *substance* of what he's trying to communicate. Why do you have to be a different person when you are giving a presentation than you are in "real life"? The answer to that question should be obvious. You don't! In fact, to try and do so will get in the way of giving your audience a great presentation.

I think we all need to have the courage to share ourselves with our audiences, warts and all. The growing trend toward "packaging" has led to a lot of disillusionment and skepticism. I'm not saying that you shouldn't set a strategy for getting across a message—that is an extremely important effort. What I'm talking about is focusing on form rather than substance.

THE BIG AUDIENCE

All of the communication tools we've been discussing are available for you to adapt to the particulars of your public speaking situation. But you may be concerned that your audience is too large for you to be able to use all of them successfully. There are certain things to keep in mind when you're facing a larger-than-average audience.

Let's take it row by row:

- Rows 1 to 3: Your audience can see your *eyes*. Use them.

- Rows 4 to 10: The audience is too far away to see your eyes but they can see your *face*. Smile a bit more broadly and turn your full face as you speak so that each part of the audience can see you.

- Rows 10 to 1,000: They can no longer see your face but they can see your *body*. Make your gestures larger, speak louder, smile broadly, and frown more obviously.

In other words:

#22 **The bigger the audience, the bigger your gestures, facial expressions, and body movements must be.**

Before you decide that I am trying to trick you into becoming an actor, consider this. If you are truly tuned in to your audience, if you are truly interested in being of real value to them, if you truly want to do a great job for them, then an amazing thing happens as the size of an audience grows: you grow with them *automatically*!

It becomes a symbiotic relationship. You see it all the time at rock concerts where the band will play for hours on end, without a break, sweating bullets, on the edge of exhaustion, but still wanting more. Meanwhile, 50,000 fans are clapping, singing along, dancing on their chairs, and screaming their lungs out. The band and the crowd are like two entities feeding on one another, creating more energy together than they ever could individually. Everyone is having a great time. The same is true for the great preachers, like Billy Graham, who can move huge audiences to uplifting experiences.

So, connect with your audience, enjoy the wonder of the experience. You have been given the great honor of leading a group for a period of time. Give them your best and do not hesitate to accept their energy in return.

Every great communicator in history has known these things and used them effectively. Some have accomplished great good; others have used communication for evil ends.

We have all read about the great speeches of Franklin Delano Roosevelt and Winston Churchill as they tried to inspire their countries during the dark days of World War II. They were both wonderful communicators. Yet the most effective of the leaders at that moment in history was probably the worst predator ever to stalk the planet. His name was Adolf Hitler.

Hitler understood the power of oral communication. He believed that a person could have a much greater impact on the cause he was supporting with the spoken word than the written word. He even put together a picture book on how to deliver a great speech. It is full of pictures of der führer posing to demonstrate his style.

The best, or most disturbing, example of his speaking effectiveness was the famous Nuremberg Stadium speech in 1934. There are more than 100,000 people in the stadium and at least that many outside. Hitler is introduced. He approaches the microphone, looks down, and says *nothing*.

If you want to get an inkling of the power Hitler had over his audiences, check out the documentary film Triumph of the Will, made by director Leni Riefenstahl at Hitler's request. Considered the greatest propaganda film ever made, the movie records the 1934 Nuremberg rally.

He is waiting for the crowd to become absolutely silent. Minutes go by, some say as many as ten, certainly a good five, of nothing. He begins to speak, softly, very softly, like the opening movement of a great symphony. The crowd leans forward, straining their ears to hear what their leader is saying.

As he continues, his voice grows louder, he turns his body to the side, and he raises his right hand, bringing it straight out to the side. He begins to punctuate his words by lifting the outstretched arm upward and forcefully bringing it down to a series of loud points he makes, one after the other, in rapid succession.

He turns now, full face to the audience, his voice rising to shouts as his right hand is now raised above his head. He hammers his hand down as he overwhelms his audience with a tidal wave of anger, hatred, and revenge. He reaches a huge bellowing climax and the crowd explodes into thunderous cheers, song, and chants of *Heil Hitler*! (Does this remind you of a rock concert?)

Hitler is now still as he waits for the silence to return so he can begin the second movement of this frightening symphony of persuasion. *We must never forget what followed.*

You see, this is why we must all work to develop our communication skills. It will help us spot those who would lead us down the wrong path by understanding their technique. It will help us to effectively challenge them and defend ourselves when we are challenged.

 Today the opportunities for communication are more abundant than at any other time in human history. None of us can afford to miss the opportunity to help others through effective communication. To do it well will require all the tools we have available to us. That is really the value of this book—to give you the freedom to use the tools available to you and the joy of having a positive impact on your audiences.

CHAPTER **3**

Writing Great Presentations

You have just been introduced to an audience by a very formal sourpuss. The person went through your credentials as if he were reading the ingredients on the side of a soup can. You're extremely annoyed at the old guy's attitude, but you're even more upset about the audience. They look like a group of Bulgarian Olympic judges.

As you look down at your notes, you notice they are a mutant cross between a manuscript and an outline. There are little messages written all over the margins. Much of the opening has been crossed out because you decided to change it at the last minute, *literally* the last minute. You have written a new opening in the little space above where you crossed out the old one. You have used abbreviations, partial words, and symbols known to you only at the moment you scribbled them.

As you examine the notes, you realize that you can't remember what the new opening was going to be. The scribbles only confuse you further. Even worse, you can't remember what the *old* opening was! You look up at the audience and smile.

They look back at you expectantly. You notice one or two of them smiling hungrily at you. You know that they know that *you* know that *they* know that you're deep in it. Soon one of them will say: "Can we get on with this?" or "Who *is* this person?" or "Are you going to talk to us, or are we supposed to pick this stuff up telepathically?"

What happens next? You get eaten alive.

You can't let yourself get into this situation. I have, and believe me, it's an awful experience. We should all avoid creating opportunities for disaster.

#23 👉 The single best way to have a successful presentation is to prepare properly.

This may sound pretty obvious, but people rarely spend enough time preparing their presentations. Preparing a presentation or speech is a pain for most people. Everybody's busy, and writing the thing tends to get put off until the last minute. Furthermore, nobody likes to sit down and stare vacantly at a piece of paper or a computer screen with absolutely no idea of what they want to say or how they want to say it.

There is a well-known story that Lincoln composed the Gettysburg Address, the most famous speech in American history, on the back of an envelope on the way to deliver the speech. Rest assured that this is only a myth! There are several drafts of the speech in existence, some of which can be dated back at least a week before the address was given.

Organization is the key. It is very clear to me that one of the main reasons people give poor speeches or presentations, besides laziness and procrastination, is an inability to organize thoughts into a clear and cohesive style.

Here's an effective way to do this. I call it the Hook, the Line, and the Sinker.

THE HOOK

The Hook is a statement designed to capture the audience's attention. If you can't get anybody to listen to you, you might as well be talking to the wall. People's attention spans today are remarkably short. There have been lots of studies done on the subject and they all reach this conclusion. You have to get your audience's attention, or you're dead in the water before you start.

Here are some ways to "Hook" your audience.

THE DRAMATIC STATEMENT

"Good morning, everyone. I appreciate the opportunity to be with you today. I am here to talk to you about a problem that, should it remain unsolved, will have a direct and serious impact on every person in this room!"

A statement like this will usually cause most people in the audience to pay attention. But please do not expect *awed* or *rapt* attention. The audience is not going to look up at you and say "Oh, joy of joys! Our speaker is beginning!" You'll most likely get a "Huh?" or an "OK, what's this all about?" or even a "Just a second, I want to hear what this person is saying" to the person next to them who was saying something as you began.

All you are trying to do with your opening is to get the audience to stop thinking about what they were thinking about and to start paying attention to you. A dramatic statement will do the trick.

By the way, I gave you an example of a scary dramatic statement. You can use positive dramatic statements just as effectively. Here's an example:

"Good afternoon, everyone. I am absolutely delighted to have the opportunity to be with all of you today. I want to tell you about some wonderful news that has just come to my attention."

This opening will work just as well as the scary one.

THE JOKE

A joke can be a great way to Hook an audience. If done properly, it can loosen up the group and the speaker, allowing them to laugh together before getting on to the business of the presentation.

If you are going to use jokes, however, it is absolutely necessary that you keep a few things in mind. First of all, be brutally honest with yourself: are you any good at telling jokes? Some people are great at telling jokes and others aren't. If you get giggles and laughs at lunch, parties, and just sitting around, then by all means go ahead and use a joke to Hook your audience.

However, if you tend to forget punch lines, or lose the premise of the joke, or have a bizarre sense of humor that only you can understand, then *don't tell jokes*. Starting a presentation with your favorite joke even though you absolutely stink at telling it is very dangerous. Your big punch line could easily be met with utter silence or the sound of crickets.

Not only does that kind of response screw up the beginning of your presentation by embarrassing the heck out of you, it makes the audience feel sorry for you or think you're a moron. Or worse.

Even if you're a fantastic joke teller, there are still things to look out for. If you *can* tell jokes, make sure they are not offensive to the audience. Keep in mind that just about any joke is potentially offensive, so be careful. I try to use self-deprecating humor where *I* am the butt of the joke. This way I'm the only person I'm offending, and I can handle it.

But be careful. Using self-deprecating humor is still risky. If you call yourself an idiot enough times, the audience may start to think you really are one, which may have a negative impact on your credibility. This has never daunted politicians, but I don't think it's a very good policy for most of us.

Another form of humor is called situational humor. This consists of little one-liners involving someone you know in the audience or something that has occurred at the meeting before or during your presentation. For instance, a speaker who was on before you totally blows a joke, and everybody has been kidding him about it. When you start your presentation, you could say something like: "I had been planning to start my presentation off with a great joke, but our previous speaker already told it."

Situational humor can also be very effective in meetings where things are getting a little intense. Sometimes a well-placed, good-natured one-liner can make everyone laugh. This is like hitting the Reset button; it dissolves the tension and allows the meeting to continue in a more positive environment. Negotiators often use this trick to buy time and change subjects.

Strong negotiating skills can be very useful when you are interacting with an audience. Two great books on the subject of negotiating:

- *You Can Negotiate Anything by my friend Herb Cohen will give you great insight into the business world. Herb is one of the funniest, brightest people I know, and he gives you some of the best negotiating techniques around.*
- *Negotiate Smart by Nicholas Reid Schaffzin (part of our Princeton Review series) offers successful negotiating strategies for a variety of situations. Everything you need to know is included, from buying your first car to closing that all-important deal, with negotiating scenarios to practice on.*

A final thing to keep in mind when you're using jokes is that they must be relevant to the presentation. Nothing sounds dumber than a speaker cracking one or two gratuitous jokes that have absolutely nothing to do with his talk, and then grinding gears as he tries to find a segue into his presentation. Stick with jokes that relate to your topic.

The Story

Telling a story is one of the most effective ways of illustrating a point. (In fact, I've been using this technique as we've been going along.) Stories can be about personal experiences, or those of family members or acquaintances. They can be inspirational or motivating in nature, involving celebrities or well-known figures in history. They can even be completely fictitious, created only to illustrate a point.

There are two major things to keep in mind if you are going to use a story as a Hook: the story must be relevant to the presentation, and it must be *brief*. Let's take a look at relevance.

I once had a truly great storyteller working for me. I don't think I've ever heard anyone spin a yarn as well as he did. He was funny, articulate, and fascinating. Whenever he conducted a seminar for one of our clients, people would compliment him on his storytelling ability. There was only one problem. The only thing the audience learned was that my associate was a great presenter and storyteller. They had not received one bit of information about how *they* might improve their presentation skills. My associate's stories were utterly irrelevant to the purpose of the presentation.

In a similar way, you can really annoy your audience if you start your presentation with a story that has absolutely nothing to do with what you have to say. If you want to use a story, make sure it ties in to the topic of your presentation.

I was once teaching a class at a large aerospace company on how to give presentations. Everyone in the class had to give a practice presentation which was videotaped and then played back for coaching purposes.

One of the people in the class was an aeronautical engineer. I asked him what he was going to talk about. He said: "I am going to discuss the aerodynamics of a wing at low level during supersonic flight. I'm going to use your Hook, Line, and Sinker stuff too."

I whispered a little prayer to myself: "Please Lord, make it *short*." Then I turned on the camera. He began:

"When I first joined the company, right out of engineering school, I had the opportunity to monitor one of the first flights of a supersonic aircraft at low level. They were trying to see how the ground avoidance equipment would work at this high speed. We had attached some sensors to the wings to see what was happening to them this close to the ground.

"I remember it was a really cold morning and the test flight kept getting delayed. We were all freezing our butts off. Then over a loudspeaker came the quiet words: 'Aircraft inbound.'

"Suddenly we picked up a flash in the sky. It was the plane and it was dropping out of the sky like a rock. Just when we thought it was going to hit the ground, the pilot pulled up and the plane headed toward us.

"It blasted right past us, rolled once, rolled again...and then crashed into the ground. The pilot never knew what hit him. We were all in complete shock.

"At that same horrible moment, the sensors we had placed on the wings were telling our computers inside the building that something terrible had happened to those wings at low level, at supersonic speeds, that caused them to stop flying.

"We have been studying this problem ever since this tragedy and I would like to give you an update on our results."

I looked around the room and saw that everybody had the same look of intense interest. *We all just had to know about the aerodynamics of a wing, at low level and supersonic speed.*

It was a tremendously compelling story that was completely relevant to the presentation—a great example of the story Hook.

Brevity is also an important issue to consider when using a story Hook. Make sure that your story doesn't take up too much of your presentation. Remember, you're just trying to get people to pay attention to you. If you go on too long with your story, you may end up boring them and losing their attention.

Now we'll look at some other kinds of Hooks.

THE LEAD-IN QUESTION

In this version of the Hook, all you have to do is ask the audience a question. It would look and sound something like this:

"Good afternoon, everyone. I am very happy to be here with all of you today. Before I start my presentation, let me ask you a question. By a show of hands, how many of you saw the State of the Union address last night?"

When you ask a lead-in question like this one, the following things will happen:

- Some people will raise their hands because they did see the address.

- Some people will not raise their hands because they did not see the address.

- Some people will raise their hands because they see other people raising their hands about something.

- Some people will ask their neighbors why people are raising their hands.

- *All* people will now start paying attention to you because they think this is going to be one of those audience participation presentations.

This little technique can be very effective if done properly. Please take note of the fact that I asked for a show of hands *before* I asked the question. If you don't do this, it's likely that people won't respond. No one wants to be the first to raise her hand if she is not sure that is what you want her to do. So ask the audience for a show of hands first, and *then* ask the question. This way you'll avoid the awful moment where there is no response from the audience.

The lead-in question has been around a long time, and it still works if you do it right.

Mentioning People in the Audience

Another way to Hook an audience is to simply mention the names of people you know who are present:

> "Good morning, everyone. I have some very interesting things to talk to you about today.
> "Mary Kukla, I know you will be particularly interested in this because you will be using it in your group. I also think that Joe Bosovani will be actively involved in refining what we will be suggesting."

At this moment, you have the undivided attention of Mary Kukla and Joe Bosovani because you are speaking about them. You have also struck fear into the hearts of everybody else in the audience. They will all be thinking to themselves: "My God, she's calling on people!" No one wants to be in the position of having his name mentioned and being caught zoning out somewhere. It embarrasses the heck out of everyone. So the audience will pay attention, at least for a while.

College professors use this trick all the time, so I'm sure it sounds very familiar to many of you. It's a nice, sneaky way to Hook an audience.

THE VISUAL HOOK

This technique involves using an interesting picture or graphic to capture the audience's attention. For instance, if you were talking about drunk driving you might show a picture of a child who was killed in a drunk-driving accident.

Another visual Hook might be a bar chart that shows a dramatic increase or decrease in revenues. All you have to do is point at the visual and say: "This is what I am going to talk to you about today." People will pay attention to this, since the information in the chart will most likely affect their chances of receiving a fat Christmas bonus this year.

All of the Hooks I've described work well with different audiences. Have fun creating your own examples of these tried-and-true techniques. They will help you to capture your audience's attention and build some confidence at the beginning of the presentation. You'll also be able to have a little fun writing your own great presentations.

Now that you have your audience's attention, you should have something worthwhile to tell them. This leads us to the second component of a great presentation.

THE LINE

The Line is your pitch. It is what you are going to talk about. In order for it to be effective, it's terribly important that it flow logically and smoothly. Here is how to put together your Line:

1. **Establish the problem or issue in general.** This may only be a sentence or two. It is simply a very general introduction to your topic. Here is an example of a Hook and the beginning of a Line:

The Hook:

"Good afternoon, everyone! Thank you for this chance to be with you today. I am here to talk about a problem that, should it remain unsolved, will have a direct and serious impact on everyone in this room!"

The beginning of the Line:

"The problem I am referring to is the continuous, unrelenting increase in our health care costs."

This Line is a short description of what you are going to talk about. Everyone in the room now knows this is what you want to discuss.

Once you have let everybody know what the problem or issue is in general, you go to the next part of the Line.

2. **Tell the audience what the components of the problem or issue are.** In other words, tell them what the things are that make it a problem or issue. This a very critical part of the Line because it helps everyone understand the problem or issue the way *you* understand it. They may not agree with your analysis, and that is perfectly OK. All you want to do at this point is have them *understand* it.

So, to continue with our example:

"As you know, the cost of health care has gone up enormously over the last five years. The debate over a National Health Insurance Program will continue in Congress well into the future. Every state in the Union has a different approach to dealing with the problem. The tremendous amount of litigation continues to drive up malpractice insurance rates for health care providers, which is passed on to all of us.

"All this litigation has also brought about the practice of 'defensive medicine' where doctors are ordering very expensive and unnecessary patient tests, just to protect themselves from future malpractice claims. In the meantime, families are going without health insurance, and companies are facing enormous costs as they attempt to provide for their employees."

I'm depressed.

But at least I know that my audience understands the seriousness of the problem and its far-reaching impacts. If they do not understand the problem or issue clearly, they will have a great deal of trouble agreeing on what to do about it. So, make sure you clearly define the components of the problem or issue you are addressing.

After you have done this you can move to the next part of the Line.

3. **Give the audience a solution or alternative solutions to the problem you are addressing (or an approach or alternative approaches to the issue you are discussing).** Now, here is something important to think about if there is more than one solution or approach to the problem or issue: if you don't care which solution or approach your audience chooses, then how you list them is irrelevant.

However, in most of the presentations you give there will be one solution or approach that you think is best. If that is the case, then you have to decide how to position it. Should it go first, somewhere in the middle, or last? Let's take a look at these alternatives.

If you put your solution first, you may confuse the heck out of your audience if you don't present it properly. By the time you get through the other alternatives your audience will have forgotten what you said about the first one.

If you put your solution in the middle of the list it will completely lose its impact. It will be hidden among the other alternatives, and everyone will have to guess what the right answer is. Remember, you are trying to help your audience understand your point of view, not engage them in a guessing game.

I think your best bet is to save your solution or approach for last. Remember the old axiom: *last heard, first remembered.*

Another nice thing about saving your solution or approach for last is that it allows you to set up the other alternatives and knock them down as you lead your audience to your conclusion. This is a very effective technique. There are exceptions to this approach, however. For example, the decision maker of the group might have to leave early. In business, this happens all the time. In this situation, I suggest that you give your solution or approach first *and* last. In this scenario you will use your Hook, do the first two parts of the Line, and then say something like this:

> *"So, that is the problem we are all facing. Now I know, Ms. Nergleman, that you will have to leave our meeting shortly. So I want you to know that I recommend that we deal with our problem with alternative number four.*

> *"This alternative calls for a joint effort on the part of our employees and management to develop a workable sharing of our health care costs. It is the fairest and most cost-effective way to deal with this very difficult situation. It is also reflective of your vision for our company.*

"I also want you to know that we examined a number of other alternative approaches, and, as your time allows, I will describe them to you and the rest of the group."

Now you can start talking about the other alternatives. In a few minutes Nergleman will split, and you can continue your discussion of the other alternatives. At the end, you can restate your thoughts about your alternative.

If Nergleman had any questions, she would have raised them at the time you first brought up your point. If she didn't tell you that you were full of baloney at that time, you're home free. Addressing the other alternatives lets everyone else know that you've fully thought out the problem. It gives you the best chance of getting agreement with your position.

Now, as you lay out your various alternative solutions, you will want to be sure to give their pluses and minuses. In our health care presentation it might look something like this:

"Now, there are a number of ways we might deal with this very serious problem. First, we could simply ignore it. This is exactly what we have been doing for the last fifty years. With any luck, Congress will eventually come up with something and the issue will be resolved.

"The drawback to this approach is that we have already tried it and nothing has happened. It doesn't work. Costs continue to escalate and growing numbers of people are living in fear of getting sick, because they have no insurance!"

You will use the same sort of approach for the other alternatives. Give the idea, say what is good about it, and then blow it sky high. Then, when you get to your solution or approach, you will be in a very strong position to support it. You can even suggest that while there are possible problems with your position, it is still the *best* of the available choices.

The nice thing about this approach is that it will force you to think honestly through the alternatives. This will result in a well-considered and genuinely worthwhile conclusion that will be very persuasive with your audience. This approach will save you a lot of time, and will give you a simple, straightforward way to provide your audiences with interesting and thoughtful information that has the important elements of credibility and persuasiveness.

Now it's time to bring the presentation to a close. This is where most people blow all their great work out their ears.

THE SINKER

The Sinker is simply this: tell the audience what you want them to *do* with the information you have given them. Have you ever been to a presentation and wondered why the speaker has told you all this stuff? I have, and it always drives me crazy. Why in the hell did this guy just tell me about all these things? What does he want me to do about them? It's just like reading a great book and finding out at the last minute that somebody has torn out the last few pages. Or like having a videotape snap just before the end of a great movie. Or going to the doctor and having him read you all the results of your tests and then simply walk out of the examining room.

Don't make audiences guess. If you do, one of two things usually happens. Either they don't guess, or they guess wrong.

No matter what it is, let your listeners know what they are supposed to do next. Sometimes you will want them to do something and sometimes you will want them to do absolutely nothing. It doesn't make any difference, as long as everybody knows that that's what you want.

Let's take a look at some examples.

If you want them to approve of what you have told them, as we do in our health care example, say something like this:

> *"So, ladies and gentlemen, in conclusion, I would like permission to proceed on the development of a fair and equitable cost-sharing plan that will provide the kind of health care all of us need at a price we all can afford!"*

Your listeners know what you want from them. They know what will happen next, and there is no room for confusion. It is a good Sinker.

If you want an audience to *delay* a decision, say something like this:

> *"So, you can see that there is still a great deal we do not know about this critical issue. Therefore, I am asking you today to hold your decision for thirty days. This will give us the time we need to study the issue further and provide you with the information you need to make a much higher quality decision."*

This is a clear and straightforward Sinker. Your listeners don't have to try to figure out what you want them to do. You just told them.

If you simply want them to look upon you as a credible source of information in the future, tell them this:

> "I hope you have found this information useful. I also hope that, should you need any other information about this issue in the future, you will look upon me and my organization as a credible source of that information."

This is the sincere Sinker. As George Burns said about sincerity: "If you can fake that, you've got it made!" All kidding aside, in this Sinker you are trying to be helpful to the audience and are asking for their trust and support in the future. It is a worthwhile thing to do and a perfectly honest and reasonable request.

If you want the audience to do *absolutely* nothing, then try this Sinker:

> *"Thank you very much for the wonderful opportunity to speak with you today. It is not necessary for you to do a thing today about the information we have discussed.*
>
> *"I wanted you all to be aware of it because I honestly believe it will be valuable information you will need to accomplish your objectives."*

Now as people leave the room they know they don't have to do a damn thing with the information. This will free them to simply appreciate it for its intrinsic value. Believe me, they will be grateful that someone had the courtesy to let them know what was expected of them.

So, there you have it. The Hook, the Line, and the Sinker.

THE BASIC HOOK, LINE, AND SINKER MODEL

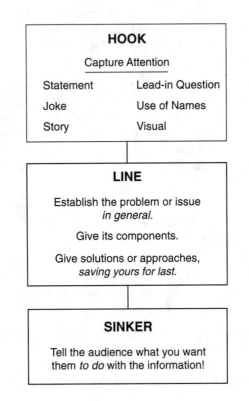

The model I have just shown you works well with a wide variety of informational or persuasive presentations. You will notice, however, that it is geared toward presentations that cover only one main subject. Every now and then, you will be asked to talk about two or three different or related subjects in the same presentation.

For example, say you are asked to give a presentation about three major sports in the United States. For the purposes of this example, we'll use *my* favorite sports, baseball, football, and basketball.

First, start with a super Hook that will grab the audience's attention *and* introduce the subjects. For example:

"Hello, everyone! I am here today to talk to you about three of the most controversial, expensive, and emotional experiences any of us will ever encounter."

Then continue the Line with this:

"I am referring to the three most popular spectator sports in the USA. They are baseball, football, and basketball."

Now you break the presentation into three parts. Each part will be a Line itself. In each of these Lines you will lay out the components of the issues surrounding each sport and some suggestions for dealing with them.

All of this will be followed by a super Sinker that will let your listeners know what you want them to do with the information you have presented.

Here's a schematic of what the presentation would look like:

THE MULTISUBJECT HLS MODEL

```
                    ┌─────────────────────────┐
                    │      SUPER HOOK         │
                    │    Grabs Attention      │
                    │   Introduces Subjects   │
                    └─────────────────────────┘
                              │
                    ┌─────────────────────────┐
                    │         LINE            │
                    │   Names Subject Areas   │
                    └─────────────────────────┘
                              │
        ┌──────────────┬──────────────┬──────────────┐
   ┌──────────┐   ┌──────────┐   ┌──────────┐
   │SUBJECT 1 │   │SUBJECT 2 │   │SUBJECT 3 │
   │Components│   │Components│   │Components│
   │Solutions │   │Solutions │   │Solutions │
   └──────────┘   └──────────┘   └──────────┘
        └──────────────┴──────────────┘
                    ┌─────────────────────────┐
                    │     SUPER SINKER        │
                    └─────────────────────────┘
```

If you want to, you can have "mini-Sinkers" after each subject Line. These let the audience know what you might want them to do with each specific set of information. It is a nice touch and can add to the clarity of your points. But remember, you will still need a super Sinker at the end of the entire presentation to bring everything to a close.

Transitions

Now that we've talked a bit about organization, we need to discuss the "glue" that holds the presentation together.

Transitions are literary devices that help you go from one point or subject to another. There are many ways to use these, but my favorite is the question transition. To execute a question transition, all you have to do is ask yourself a question.

How does it work?

There. I just used one. Let me show you how the question transition works in conjunction with the Hook, Line, and Sinker:

"Good afternoon, everyone. Thanks for the opportunity to be with you today.

"Well, why are we here?

"We are meeting today to discuss a problem that will have a tremendous impact on everyone here.

"What is the problem I am referring to?"

Tell the audience what the problem is.

"What are the components of the problem? What makes it such a problem?"

Tell them what the components of the problem are.

"What are we going to do about this terrible problem?"

Give them a solution or alternative solutions to the problem, *saving yours for last.* You can do this with another question transition after you've laid out the alternative solutions.

"What do I think we should do?"

Tell them what your solution is.

"Why do I believe this is our best alternative?"

Tell them why you do, then go to your Sinker:

"Finally, ladies and gentlemen, what do I need from you?"

Tell them what you want them to do with the information.

Now, I am a very big fan of the question transition for a number of reasons. First, if you are truly focused on helping the audience understand an important problem or issue, then question transitions can be the very questions the audience would ask you if you were just having coffee together.

Second, because you're asking questions, you'll answer in your own words. This will make you more conversational, loosen you up a bit, and make you much easier to listen to and to watch.

Third, there will be times when you'll have to discuss controversial issues, and you might be challenged by people in the audience. The challenges usually come in the form of questions.

In these situations, an interesting phenomenon often takes place. The night before the presentation you wake up in a cold sweat and say to yourself:

"My God! I hope they don't ask me *this* tomorrow!"

At precisely the same moment someone who is going to attend your presentation and wants to challenge you wakes up and says to herself:

"Eureka! I'll ask him *this* tomorrow!"

This amazing phenomenon has led me to this very important pointer:

> **#24** 👉 **If you are reasonably sure that a difficult subject is going to come up during your presentation, raise it yourself in the form of a question transition.**

I don't know how to quantify "reasonably sure", but I do know how it feels at a gut level. I think you will have a gut-level feeling yourself. The important thing to remember here is that you'll want to deal with the issue *offensively* (in the best sense of the word).

Unfortunately, most people in this situation decide that they will wait and see if the issue comes up. When it does, they find themselves in the compromising situation of having to deal with it *defensively*. The question transition will help you avoid this kind of problem.

By the way, if you are not particularly thrilled with using the Hook, Line, and Sinker in conjunction with the question transition, consider using the question transition by itself. Say you are going to give a presentation on a research project you have been conducting. You could easily lay out your presentation as follows:

> *"Good morning, everyone. I am here today to discuss my research project, in which I attempted to answer the following questions:*
>
> *"What are the appropriate boundaries of my study?*
>
> *"What techniques should be used to conduct the study?*
>
> *"What did I discover?*

"How do I know that my results are accurate?

"What needs to be done with the results?

"This morning, I will answer those questions for you and then answer any questions you might have about my project."

Then all you have to do is answer the questions, one at a time.

I like this approach because it cuts through all the flowery stuff and gets right to the meat of the presentation.

So, that is the question transition. I hope you find it useful, with or without the Hook, Line, and Sinker.

There are other ways to make transitions in a presentation. Another one of my favorites is the trigger-word transition. In this type, you mention a word near the end of your first point or subject and then repeat it in the first sentence of your next point or subject. It looks like this:

*"So, you can see that there are still many aspects of the stars that remain **mysteries** to us.*

*"And speaking of **mysteries**, consider the vast unknown of the ocean depths that we are just beginning to discover."*

This is another easy way to get out of one subject and into another. You can also use the direct approach to transitions by simply saying things like:

"Now let's talk about..."

"Turning to our next issue..."

"Another significant point to be made is..."

"Here's a significant thing to remember..."

I had a guy in one of my classes who could never come up with a transition, so he would simply say "Switching!" Worked for him. Whatever.

 So, now we've talked about organizing a presentation. I hope the Hook, Line, and Sinker will help you organize your presentations quickly and efficiently and perhaps even allow you to enjoy what you're doing.

Choosing a Presentation Format

As you already know, there's more than one way to skin a cat. There are also several ways to build and deliver a presentation. In this chapter we'll examine the four major types of presentations: the written manuscript presentation, the memorized presentation, the ad-lib presentation, and the outline presentation. I'll give you the pluses and minuses of each, and you can decide which format is best for you.

THE WRITTEN MANUSCRIPT PRESENTATION

The written manuscript presentation is a fully scripted speech. Every word and number you'll deliver to your audience is written down on paper. This format is, by far, the safest way to give a presentation, for obvious reasons. All of the language is right in front of you. All of the statistical data are there to be read. You have a logical sequence to follow. You have a track to run on.

All you have to do is *read* to the audience. On the surface, it seems that a semimoron should be able to get through this type of presentation—that is, if you believe that presentations should be read and not heard.

In fact, appearances to the contrary, the written manuscript presentation is, by far, the single most *difficult* way to deliver a presentation. The reason is clear. If it's not done properly, it robs you of the levels of communication with your audience we discussed earlier. You get locked into a series of words and phrases, and lose yourself worrying so much about *what* you're saying that you lose sight of *how* you're saying it. It can turn a bright, interesting person into a boring, monotonous presenter.

Now let's talk about delivering a written manuscript presentation.

I want to turn first to the worst possible case: *the manuscript was written for you by someone else.* This is a bad situation because you're being asked to deliver material that's not your own. The person who wrote this presentation may not see the world the same way you do. He may not express himself the way you express yourself. Therefore, before you can deliver this kind of presentation, *you must make it your own.*

Here's how:

Read the presentation from beginning to end
What is it saying, where is it going, and how is it getting there? Does it make any sense? Is it logical? Is it what you want to say? In other words, plug into the *intellectual level* of the presentation.

Read the presentation paragraph by paragraph
Your job is to determine the emotional set of each paragraph. When you have done so, write yourself a *one-word note* in the margin expressing the appropriate *emotional* response.

For instance, the opening line of the presentation might read: "Good morning, ladies and gentlemen, it's a pleasure to be with you today." The emotional set of this paragraph might be *"friendly"* or *"courteous."* Write one of these words in the margin. Jot down a new word each time the emotional response changes.

Remember that you're writing only one-word notes, *not* phrases. The reason is compelling. I've found that writing more than one word in the margin often causes the presenter to read the sentences out loud. This can be embarrassing.

Read the presentation word by word
You're looking for two kinds of words. The first are emotional, action, sensual, and descriptive words and numbers. You'll need a fine-tip black felt pen. Underline those words or numbers you want to deliberately intensify. If you want to throw a word or number

away, put it in parentheses. This will remind you to *stretch* and *compress* in the appropriate places. Here's an example:

> For a (\$5,000) investment, you will receive a <u>\$10,000</u> profit.

The second kind of words to look for are words you'll consistently trip over during the presentation. When you find one of these, change it to a word you won't have so much trouble with. Brilliant suggestion, no? However, there is a pitfall, which leads to another suggestion: if you change a word, make sure that you have not changed the intended meaning of the sentence. Finally, be sure to check your changes with a friend, your boss, or, if necessary, your lawyer.

When you get done working with the presentation you should end up with something that looks like this (the slash marks are where you will take a pause—one slash for a quick pause, two slashes for a longer pause):

> <u>Good</u> <u>morning,</u> everyone./ I <u>appreciate</u> the <u>opportunity</u> to be with you today.//
>
> I am here today to talk to you about a <u>problem</u>/ that, should it remain <u>unsolved,</u>/ will have a <u>direct</u> and <u>serious</u> impact on <u>every</u> person in this <u>room</u>!//

You will now have read the presentation several times. Read it again and again, until you're able to pick up *two lines* of copy at a time and speak them out to the audience. In other words, until you've achieved total mastery of the material.

This approach is time consuming, so keep that in mind when you're selecting a presentation format. However, there may be times when you're asked to deliver an important speech in this manner, in which case you're going to have to bite the bullet. Just make certain that you control the material, rather than allowing it to control you.

THE MEMORIZED PRESENTATION

Another way to deliver a written presentation is to memorize it and recite it for the audience. The memorized presentation has all the benefits of the written manuscript presentation as far as language, data, and sequencing go. By all means use the memorized presentation if you have all three of the following qualities: you have a photographic memory, you do not get nervous when you give a presentation, and you work extremely well under pressure.

If you're missing any one of these three qualities, I suggest that you pass on the memorized presentation. A brief story might help make the point here.

I was in Anchorage, Alaska, for two weeks conducting seminars. When it came time to return home, I discovered that the only flight to Los Angeles left at 1:00 A.M. So I had some time to kill. I began to imagine the airplane flying over frozen mountains and gigantic icebergs. This began to make me nervous. I decided to visit the airport bar to fortify myself for the journey. I kept thinking about the icebergs which, in turn, caused me to continue fortifying. By the time I got on the airplane I was reasonably relaxed. In other words, I was smashed. Now, I'm a bit of a wise guy naturally, and the fortifying did not help.

We began to taxi and the flight attendant started her instruction. It went something like this:

> "Good evening, ladies and gentlemen, and welcome to Flight 684 to Seattle and Los Angeles. In order to familiarize yourself with our aircraft, I would like to ask you to look at the information card in the seat-back pocket in front of you."

I looked for the information card, but I just couldn't find it. I'm not saying it wasn't there. I just couldn't find it. I did find the little magazine they give you and some person's ticket from a previous flight. But I had no luck with the information card. So, I said, rather loudly: "I haven ga one!"

The flight attendant immediately interrupted her instructions, which were, of course, *memorized*. She pulled the microphone away from her face and said, "I beg your pardon, sir?"

I replied, "I haven ga an informashun car in th seebakpoketinfroname! An if this sucker goes down I wanna know howtagetoff!!"

The flight attendant grimaced, opened a little cabinet, pulled out an information card, and handed it to me.

She then put the microphone to her lips to continue her instructions. She pushed the button activating the microphone and got a puzzled look on her face. The expression lasted a good five seconds and melted into a nervous shrug. She then said:

> "Good evening, ladies and gentlemen, and welcome to Flight 684..."

By this time, just about everyone on the plane was laughing, including the flight attendant. After her pitch she came over to me with a big grin and informed me that she would not let me have another drink all the way to L.A. We did, however, work it out: I got plenty of coffee and cookies.

There are lots of good books on improving your memory. My personal favorite is The Memory Book *by former basketball great Jerry Lucas and Harry Lorayne.*

The point of this little story is, you don't want to be in the middle of an important presentation, get interrupted, and have to go all the way back to the beginning.

THE AD-LIB PRESENTATION

In the ad-lib presentation you work with no notes, no visual aids, no nothing. It's just you and your audience. The ad-lib presentation can be a wonderful vehicle for communication. If it's done well, it has the following benefits:

1. Audience involvement.
2. Excellent eye contact.
3. Spontaneity of thought.
4. Flexibility of language.

The only warning I have about this kind of presentation is that *you must know your material absolutely cold.* I don't mean a general knowledge of the information. I mean an in-depth, multifaceted grasp of the material. When you're delivering an ad-lib presentation, you need many conceptual threads available to you. If you lose one conceptual thread you should be able to pick up another *instantaneously.* If you can't, your audience will notice and your credibility will begin to erode. Not to mention that you'll likely experience a full-tilt anxiety attack.

Now, I'm sure that there are many subjects you do have an in-depth conceptual grasp of. However, if you must give presentations about subjects with which you're somewhat less familiar, then consider the outline presentation.

THE OUTLINE PRESENTATION

The outline presentation shares a lot of the benefits of other types of presentations.

1. Clear language.

2. Accurate statistical data.

3. A logical sequence.

4. Spontaneity.

5. Flexibility.

6. Audience involvement.

All of these things can be yours with the outline presentation, *if* you do it properly. Let's use a thirty-minute presentation as an example. I've seen outlines for thirty-minute presentations that run fifteen pages long. There is no way in the world that you are going to get through fifteen pages of outline material in thirty minutes. In fact, outlines of this length can take two or three hours to deliver.

So, here's how to create a thirty-minute outline presentation.

First, find a quiet work area.

Second, using whatever outline format you prefer—Roman numerals, letters, or numbers—start to lay out your presentation. Many word-processing programs have built in outliners. Check if yours does—this may be a big timesaver! You'll find the question transition used in conjunction with Hook, Line, and Sinker very helpful here. When you've laid it all out you'll probably have as much as six pages of material.

Third, *cut the material back.*

Ask yourself: "Do I really need this point written down? Or can I use a word or phrase to get me through it?" What you're headed for ideally is *either* one 8 1/2-by-11-inch piece of paper or five or six 3-by-5-inch cards.

"I carry fire insurance, but I don't expect my house to burn down."

—Winston Churchill, when asked why he carries notes to speeches but never uses them

---

On the 8 1/2-by-11-inch paper you should end up with five or six major trigger words or phrases. These trigger words or phrases are the big conceptual threads of your presentation. They may end up being the question transitions themselves.

In addition, for each major trigger word or phrase, you'll have two or three subordinate trigger words or phrases. These subordinate trigger words or phrases will help you get through complex concepts and will keep you on track.

Finally, you'll include any critical statistical data that are appropriate to each trigger word or phrase. To determine which statistical data are critical, ask yourself: if there were *one* number I want my audience to remember, what would it be? Then write that number down on the outline so you don't forget it when you actually give the presentation.

Did you notice the order in which I discussed the four different presentation formats? I presented the pluses and minuses of each, ending with my favorite, the outline presentation. As I mentioned in chapter three, this is how I recommend that you organize your presentations for maximum impact.

If you are using 3-by-5-inch cards, consider the following:

On each 3-by-5-inch card you will have one major trigger word or phrase, two or three subordinate trigger words or phrases, and any attendant critical statistical data.

In either case, keep the notes out of your hand, where they will simply be a distraction. If you're using 3-by-5-inch cards it can actually be dangerous to hold on to them. If you're interrupted during your presentation by a question or comment, you may unconsciously shuffle the stack of cards. You'll get a chilly sensation down your spine when you attempt to make your next point and find that it has disappeared into the deck.

 Think about the pros and cons of each presentation format as you decide which one is best for you. Remember, there is no such thing as a presentation for all occasions. The key is to select an appropriate format, then get down to some serious preparation.

CHAPTER 5

Visual Aids: From the Stupid to the Stellar

Most people use visual aids for the *wrong* reasons, making them crutches for their presentations. Visual aids can be marvelous vehicles for copping out. Let's face it, if you put together a great big stack of visual aids, you don't have to worry about what you are going to say. All you have to do is read the visual aids to your audience. Furthermore, if you do a lousy job, you can always blame it on the graphics department.

People misuse visual aids because they really don't understand the function of a visual aid. To me, a visual aid is very clearly defined by its *name*. It is a *visual aid* to a presentation. It is not the presentation.

There is an important relationship between a speaker and her visual aids. If the visual aid is so complex, so convoluted, that it overpowers you, then you become nothing more than a projectionist. Being a projectionist is an honorable profession, but it is not the task you have been asked to perform. On the other hand, if the visual aid is so silly, so useless, that the speaker completely overpowers it, then you have to ask the obvious question: "Why did you have a visual aid in the first place?"

There are two good reasons to use a visual aid:

1. Use a visual aid to communicate information that is too complex to communicate verbally. Certainly, it's a lot easier to explain the inner workings of a computer system, or the flow of an organization, or a numerical formula with a visual aid than to try to do it on your fingers.

2. Use a visual aid for visual impact. Visual aids can be wonderful devices for showing the majesty of an airplane in flight, or the beauty of a new building, or to graphically demonstrate the complexity of a system. But it's crucial that you *use* visual aids, not *abuse* them.

Now that we're clear on when to use or not use a visual aid, let's talk about the format of visual aids. The cardinal rule is that:

A visual aid should never stand on its own.

If it stands on its own, it is a presentation, not a visual aid.

I just love to attend a presentation where the presenter gets up, puts a paragraph on the screen, and proceeds to read it to us. Short naps are hard to come by and I appreciate the consideration. If you put paragraphs up on a screen and read them to the audience, understand that not only are you *not* communicating, you are, in fact, *preventing* communication.

Let me explain. The normal speed of human speech runs somewhere between 125 and 185 words per minute. There are people who speak faster than that, but they are exceptions. At the same time, most of us are able to read between 300 and 600 words per minute. So, if you put a paragraph up on the screen and read it to me at an average pace of, say, 150 words per minute, I can still read it *twice as fast* as you can say it.

This situation will inevitably bring on what I call the Sunday Morning Syndrome. It goes like this: it is Sunday morning. You are at home, having a cup of coffee and reading the paper. You are about halfway through an interesting article on canine aerobics when someone begins to talk to you. Eventually, you will turn to that person and say: *"What?"*

You haven't heard what was said and now you've lost what you were reading. All meaningful communication has been blocked out by distraction. Now, that may not be of tremendous importance on a cozy Sunday morning, but it can have a significant impact on the success of a presentation.

If you feel that you must put a paragraph up on the screen, for example a policy statement or a quote, first give your audience a chance to read it to themselves. Then take a moment a read it to them aloud. That way they're getting the information twice. They will have *read* it the first time and *heard* it the second time.

However, here's an even better suggestion:

Visualize rather than verbalize.

The old saying is right: a picture *is* worth a thousand words. I prefer picture visuals, *where they are appropriate*, to word visuals any day of the week. Here are some examples of picture visuals:

- Photographs
- Diagrams
- Renderings, "artist's conceptions"
- Graphs
- Bar charts
- Flow charts
- Time lines (to track progress on a project)
- Maps
- Simple schematics
- Interactive computer graphics
- Videotapes
- Anything that will graphically communicate your point

If you use a graph or diagram, make sure that it's clear and simple enough for everybody in the room to read. Also, keep any explanatory words on the visual to an absolute minimum. If a visual is too wordy, your audience will be too busy reading to spend any time listening to you.

This suggestion also applies to legends on graphs. Legends are the written explanations for specific graph lines. You don't need them: you can serve as the legend and explain what you mean. If you include a legend, we don't need you.

That does not mean that every single visual in a presentation must be picture oriented. It just means that words should be kept to a minimum. We all know that in some situations word visuals can help you make a point. So, if you've come to the conclusion that a portion of your story will be better told through a word visual, then consider the five-by-five rule.

#25 No more than five lines to any one visual. No more than five words to any one line.

That may seem like a pretty strict rule. Well, it is, so let me give you some suggestions about how to follow it when you put together word visuals.

First, visuals do not require articles (*a, the*) or prepositions (*of, from, by*). For example, the line:

The Design Criteria for the Space Shuttle

Could easily be changed to read:

Design Criteria—Space Shuttle

This says exactly the same thing *without* the articles and prepositions. You will plug them back in verbally when you are giving the presentation. Remember, you will be right next to the visual to explain what you mean.

Second, don't be afraid to move words around and remove unnecessary words to make a point while following the five-by-five rule. For instance, the line:

Define Requirements for the Engineering Building

Can be replaced with:

Engineering Building Requirements

without changing the meaning.

There is a corollary to the five-by-five rule:

#26 Stay with one major subject per visual.

If you are going to be talking about baseball, football, and basketball, don't try to explain all three games on one visual. Instead, create an introductory visual that says:

Baseball

Football

Basketball

You can then key your supporting visuals to each major title. For instance:

Baseball—Requirements

Nine Players (Ten—American League)

Four Umpires

Balls, Bats, Gloves

Field

Three Bases, Home Plate

You can even key your picture visuals to the main titles by inserting the appropriate title at the top of each picture visual.

If you attempt to discuss different subjects using the same visual, you'll confuse your audience, or worse, yourself. One subject per visual will make it easier for you to lead us through your presentation, and a heck of a lot easier for us to follow.

#27 If you don't want to talk about something, don't put it on a visual.

I've been to many, many presentations that have bombed because the speaker felt it necessary to display every analysis he went through to reach his conclusion. As a result, he ended up spending tremendous amounts of time explaining things that had little or no relevance to the final conclusion.

Put only those things that are pertinent to the discussion on a visual. If someone in the audience wants to know how you got to a particular point, let her ask! Don't lose your audience with information overkill.

You might have noticed a dovetail here between the five-by-five rule and my earlier discussion of outline presentations. Done properly, the five-by-five points can become the conceptual threads of your presentation. In other words, they will be the trigger words and phrases.

Now let's talk about three general rules for displaying visual aids. The first one is important to getting off to a good start.

#28 Always stay close to your visual aid.

This is important because it establishes for the audience an association between you and your visual aid. It will also facilitate any pointing you do during the presentation.

It's always amusing to watch a speaker stand at a lectern at one side of a room and have her visuals set up on the opposite side. She will want to point something out and will either walk all the way across the room in dead silence or will attempt to locate the data point with a long laborious description of what she is trying to get you to notice. Neither approach works. But it does add comic relief to the presentation, for the first one or two visuals, anyway. Then it becomes distracting and annoying.

Have you ever been to a presentation where the speaker stands up, puts his first visual on the screen, and then introduces himself? I have, and I never catch the poor guy's name. I am always too busy reading his first visual to listen to him. If you do what I just described, no one will know your name either. If you have spent a great deal of time and effort putting together your presentation, you will want the audience to know who you are. So don't split their attention. Save the visual aid for after you introduce yourself. This is the second rule of displaying visual aids:

#29 ☞ A visual aid should never get ahead of you.

One of your primary jobs as a presenter is to lead your audience to a conclusion, *your* conclusion. To do that, it is very important that they understand your information *your* way. If your visuals get ahead of you, the audience will invariably interpret the information *their* way, which is usually incorrect.

A visual aid should be revealed at the exact moment you are going to use it to make a point. So, keep it hidden until you are ready for it.

The next suggestion is the flip side of the last one:

#30 ☞ A visual aid should never get behind you.

When you're done with a visual aid, *get rid of it*. If you leave it in plain view of the audience, they will begin to reinterpret what you just explained. This can cause confusion and will almost always slow up the progress of your presentation.

One more thing: make sure your visual aids are clearly visible from the audience. They will do you absolutely no good if nobody can see them.

So much for the general considerations about visual aids. Next, let's talk about visual aid formats.

Dumb Visual Aids

The interview was a waste. Charlie knew that it was just a matter of time before he took another job with the city. He was tired of his basement apartment and his do-nothing burn-out girlfriend. He was tired of having to apologize for not being the young go-getter his family had expected him to become. Now, here he was leaving another defunct interview, grimly carrying his useless resume and his battered self-confidence back out onto the streets of Tempe. If only he hadn't moved. If only he hadn't taken that year off. If only, If only, If only he were Midas and gold shot out his butt on command. Karl Marx faced similar oppressions and rose above them, so where was Chuck's luck. He paused for a moment, standing there in the dirty street, obliviously scanning the remainder of his petty rash. Perhaps that slice of pizza he so desired was no longer a viable option. Another hungry lunch. The prospect of this turned his appetite to nausea. He suddenly turned, his head lolling like a swamped boat in a gale, and jettisoned a multi-colored fountain of vomit high into the air. It was quite a sight.

In crude economics you are a product, the resume is your advertisement, and the employer is the consumer. Or, if you are a recently released film, your resume is a "coming attraction," and the employer is the moviegoer. We think you get the picture. Your goal is to convince the employer that you are worth considering for a job. Your resume is one of the best ways you have to do this. It must entice, intrigue, and prove to the employer that you have the ability to get the job done. It must distinguish you from the competition. Your resume must sell you!

Because the competition is so stiff, you've got to toot your own horn. If you don't tell the employer about your skills and talents, who will? No one is going to whisper in her ear about how wonderful you are. That is your job. Of course, you must be careful not to get carried away. After all, you are not exactly a Pepsi, BMW, or a pair of Calvin Klein underwear. The fairly lax rules of advertising that apply to these products don't apply to human beings. Be reasonably honest. Make sure that the information on your resume is accurate. Even a small lie, if detected, could put a quick end to your job candidacy.

It is not unusual for an employer to receive over two hundred resumes for a single job vacancy. This allows employers to be extremely selective about granting interviews. Because the job market is an employers' market, you must write your resume with their needs in mind. First and foremost you must communicate to the employer that you have the skills and qualifications they need. Think of yourself as a problem solver. Their problem may be selling 3D glasses, providing a shuttle service to the airport, building condominiums on Mars, or revitalizing the president's image. Whatever the employer's need, your resume must convince him that you can help him fulfill that need. A well-written, precisely tailored resume can help you obtain job interviews. During the interview the resume can guide the interviewer directly to your professional strengths, particularly those that relate most closely to the position for which you are applying. After the interview, your resume remains to remind employers of your key qualifications. But the buck stops there. No resume, however outstanding, gets a job offer. You do. A resume does not speak for you, dress you suitably, shake hands firmly for you, or teach you body language techniques. Looking great on paper is important, but it mostly serves to set the tone for the main act—the interview. As they say in hockey, you must be able to finish. Just as a perfect setup is wasted if you don't score, a trashproof resume is for nought if you don't succeed at the interview.

In crude economics you are a product, the resume is your advertisement, and the employer is the consumer. Or, if you are a recently released film, your resume is a "coming attraction," and the employer is the moviegoer. We think you get the picture. Your goal is to convince the employer that you are worth considering for a job. Your resume is one of the best ways you have to do this. It must entice, intrigue, and prove to the employer that you have the ability to get the job done. It must distinguish you from the competition. Your resume must sell you! Because the competition is so stiff, you've got to toot your own horn. If you don't tell the employer about your skills and talents, who will? No one is going to whisper in her ear about how wonderful you are. That is your job. Of course, you must be careful not to get carried away. After all, you are not exactly a Pepsi, BMW is not unusual for an employer to receive over two hundred resumes for a single job vacancy. This allows employers to be extremely selective about granting interviews. Because the job market is an employers' market, you must write your resume with their needs in mind. First and foremost you must communicate to the employer that you have the skills and qualifications they need. Think of yourself as a problem solver. Their problem may be selling 3D glasses, providing a shuttle service to the airport, building condominiums on Mars, or revitalizing the president's image. Whatever the employer's need, your resume must convince him that you can help him fulfill that need. well-written, precisely tailored resume can help you obtain job interviews. During the interview the resume can guide the interviewer directly to your professional strengths, particularly those that relate most closely to the position for which you are applying. After the interview, your resume remains to remind employers of your key qualifications. But the buck stops there. No resume, however outstanding, gets a job offer. You do. A resume does not speak for you, dress you suitably, shake hands firmly for you, or teach you body language techniques. Looking great on paper is important, but it mostly serves to set the tone for the main act—the interview. As they say in hockey, you must be able to finish. Just as a perfect setup is wasted if you don't score, a trashproof resume is for nought if you don't succeed at the interview.

In crude economics you are a product, the resume is your advertisement, and the employer is the consumer. Or, if you are a recently released film, your resume is a "coming attraction," and the employer is the moviegoer. We

Magnifying glass not included.

A Horse

You're kidding.

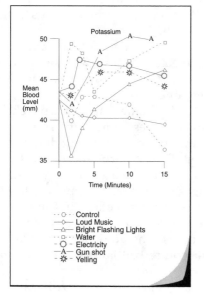

Potassium

Mean Blood Level (mm)

50
45
40
35

0   5   10   15

Time (Minutes)

- O - Control
- ◇ - Loud Music
- △ - Bright Flashing Lights
- □ - Water
- O - Electricity
- A - Gun shot
- ☼ - Yelling

We'll take your word for it.

Opponents of what may loosely be described as the "structuralist" theoretical agenda argue that these contemporary theories undermine and subjugate literature by denying its ontological mission, and by subverting—under the theoretical guise of interdisciplinary scholarship—the New Criticism's interpretive project with a multitude of diverse and often tangential discourses. This usurpation, they argue, negates the existence of a given work's discrete essence, devalues the critic's elucidative task, and ultimately denigrates the artist's creative act.

Whatever.

First, let's discuss the backbone of America's military/industrial complex:

THE OVERHEAD PROJECTOR

Different people call the overhead projector different things. Some call it a vugraph machine, others a viewfoil machine. Some people even call it a slide projector, confusing it with a 35mm projector. They are all referring to the same thing.

An overhead projector is a relatively simple contraption. It's a box with a piece of clear glass over the top. Inside the box is a very bright light. Attached to the box is an arm. On the arm is a magnifying lens which is positioned directly over the top of the box.

This box is used to display clear acetate, usually 8 1/2 by 11 inches in size, with writing or graphics or even a photograph imprinted on it. These imprinted acetates become known as "slides," "vugraphs," or "viewfoils." The slides are placed on the clear glass of the box. When the light is turned on, it reflects the image on the slide through the magnifier lens and onto a screen or wall.

With that oversimplified description of something that probably took years to perfect, let's proceed. First of all, for most overhead projector presentations the smallest type size that will be readable by your audience will be 1/4 inch. If you make the type much smaller than that you will be facing the probability that a significant portion of your audience will either be straining to see the visual or will not be able to see it at all.

A good way of determining whether your vugraph is readable is to have someone hold it up, unprojected, fifteen feet away from you. If you can read it from that distance your audience will be able to as well. If you can't, make a new one.

Second, always put your acetates in frames. You can purchase frames in the same place you got the acetates (almost any stationery or office supply store). There are a number of reasons for doing this. First, acetates tend to stick together. This is normally due to static electricity that builds up on the surfaces of the acetates. If you have them in frames they won't stick together and will be much easier to handle during the presentation. Also, putting acetates in frames can help you through complex portions of your presentations. You can use the frame as a place for extra notes. The audience won't know that you've done it and will think you're brilliant. At last, a legal use for a cheat sheet!

Now that you have prepared the vugraphs, you will want to display them properly to get the most out of them. So, here are some tips:

First, always start your overhead projection presentation with your first vugraph on the machine and the light *off*. Place the vugraph on the machine face up and readable to *you*. You don't have to worry about putting it on the machine upside down or backward. Just place it on the glass top of the box as though you were going to read it to the group without turning on the machine. Before the presentation turn the light on for a moment to adjust the focus and size of your projection. This is easily done by turning the appropriate knob on the lens holder. After you have done that, turn the machine off again to start your presentation.

Next, you will need to know how to control and direct your audience's attention to the vugraphs. There are a couple of ways to do this. They fall into two categories. You can do it at the machine, or you can do it at the screen. I'll discuss both techniques and give you their respective occupational hazards.

If you choose to control and direct from a position at the machine, you'll block the view of some people in the room. If you stand to the right of the machine, your body will be blocking the view of the people on that side. The same thing is true for the left side. So you will occasionally need to step out of the way to let them see the screen.

There are three ways to direct at the machine. There is the time-honored tradition of pointing, but you can also use the "reveal" technique or the "overlay" technique. The reveal technique can be very useful if you have a great deal of information on a vugraph. It's a good way to go when you have to work through columns of numbers, comparisons, time lines, and wordy vugraphs. It should be used as a last resort for quick and dirty presentations.

Let's assume that you've inherited a very busy vugraph from your boss. It has eight or nine points spelled out on it, the last of which is the punch line. Since you don't want your audience to see the last line right away, you place the vugraph on the machine and cover it with a piece of paper or cardboard. That way you can slide the covering down line by line during the presentation, revealing each point individually. This approach will avoid confusing your audience and you won't be giving away information before you're ready to.

There is one problem with the reveal technique. If you get more than halfway down the vugraph, the covering will fall off, making you look and feel stupid. So, here's a trick to avoid the problem. When you're preparing the presentation, take a piece of cardboard (the back of an 8 1/2-by-11-inch notepad will work nicely) and a heavy wooden ruler. Tape or glue the ruler to the top of the cardboard so that the ruler sticks out on one side. Now you have something to grab when you want to reveal the next point and the weight of the ruler will prevent the covering from falling off.

Another technique for controlling and directing an audience's attention is the overlay technique. The overlay technique is very useful for developing complex schematics, and for showing graphs, bar charts, and form samples. It can be used successfully in a variety of presentations. Here's how it works: let's assume you want to show a graph depicting sales growth from 1992 to 1994. To do this properly you'll need a baseline vugraph and three "overlays," which are additional pieces of acetate attached to the baseline.

The baseline vugraph displays only the axes of the graph with the appropriate dollars and years. The first overlay features only the graph line for 1992, the second, only the graph line for 1993, and the third only the graph line for 1994. During the presentation you start with the baseline vugraph to establish for the audience the frame of reference of your discussion. As you proceed you will overlay each graph line on the baseline. The audience will see the graph develop in front of them instead of seeing everything all at once. This technique will allow you to discuss the variables that occur from year to year one at a time and prevents any possible confusion and misinterpretation by the audience.

Now let's get on with the discussion of pointing technique.

Pointing at the Machine

Many presenters simply find the object on the vugraph they want the audience to see and point at it. That seems perfectly logical but it can present something of a problem. If you are a bit nervous, your hands may tremble slightly. That slight tremble will look like a neurological earthquake on the screen. It will magnify your anxiety and will, in turn, make you more nervous, which will make your hand tremble even more.

Here's how to beat the problem. Find the object on the vugraph you want the audience to see. Take your pointer or a pencil and rotate your hand around that object, in effect circling it. Rotating your hand will do two things for you. First, it will disguise the shaking. Since there will be two different kinds of motion, the audience will not be able to see the trembling in your hands. Second, rotating your hand will actually reduce the shaking. Trembling hands are simply a physical manifestation of a neurological disturbance brought on by anxiety. By rotating your hand you will cause a reflex reaction in your hand and arm muscles that will stabilize the shaking.

When I was a kid I had a barber named Jack. He was about eighty years old and suffered from two maladies. One was halitosis and the other was a mild case of Parkinson's disease, which caused uncontrollable shaking in Jack's extremities, most ominously his hands. Now, Jack liked to shave the back of my neck with a straight razor. When he would come at me with that thing, my entire life would pass before my eyes. He would grab my head and it would begin to shake in harmony with Jack's hand. But whenever he would hit me with that razor the shaking would stop completely! As soon as he got the razor off my neck we would start rockin' and rollin' again.

I asked my Dad about it (he's a physician) and he explained the reflex reaction to me. I tried it during my next vugraph presentation and it worked. It will work for you, too.

Some people like to beat the shaking problem by placing the pointer right on the vugraph itself. That is perfectly all right as long as you remember where you put the pointer. I have seen many people place the pointer on the vugraph and proceed to forget where they left it. As a result, they were talking about point three while the pointer was still pointing at point one. Looks dumb.

POINTING AT THE SCREEN

This is the best way to direct attention, because you're close to your visual, you're out of the way of your audience, and it's easier to maintain eye contact during the presentation. Many people have difficulty pointing at the screen, so let me show you step by step how to do it.

1. Tell the audience what you want them to find.

2. Turn and find it yourself.

3. Point at it while still looking at it. If you are using a pointer, lightly touch the screen; if not, use your index finger as your pointer.

4. While you're still looking at the point, tell the audience what they're looking at.

5. Recapture the audience's attention by looking back at them.

6. Drop your hand.

You may have been told *"Don't talk to the screen."* Please allow me to add one operative word to this suggestion. Do not talk to the screen *unnecessarily.* Here is the basic rule of thumb:

#31 👉 **If you want the audience to look at the screen, you look at it.**
If you want the audience to look at you, you look at them.

The main thing to keep in mind is that you are the recognized leader in the room. Your job is to *lead* your audience through your visual aids. If you spend all of your time looking at the visuals, so will your audience. That automatically places you in a subordinate position to the visual—not the place you want to be.

A comment or two about pointers might be helpful here. A pointer is a *pointer*. It is not a musical conductor's baton, or a sword, or a riding crop. It is a *pointer*. When you are using a pointer, it should be kept at your side when you are not pointing at something. When you are finished with it, *get rid of it!* If you don't, you'll begin to play with it unconsciously. At best, it will distract your audience. At worst, you will put someone's eye out! Neither occurrence will add to your presentation.

Incidentally, all of the pointing techniques I have just described can be applied to the other types of visual aids we'll discuss later.

THE 35mm SLIDE PRESENTATION

The 35mm slide presentation is the second most common type of presentation. The first thing to remember is that a 35mm slide should be readable at arm's length, *unprojected.* If you are unable to do so, your audience will have great difficulty seeing it during the presentation.

A 35mm slide show should always begin with the projector on, the light inside the projector on and a "blackout" slide in the chamber. A blackout slide is simply a 35mm slide with absolutely nothing on it. It is created by taking pictures with the lens cap still on the camera. I've personally created many blackout slides while on vacation with my family.

Placing a blackout slide in the chamber will let you find out if the projector and light are in good working order without distracting your audience. In addition, if there will be more than thirty to forty-five seconds between your slides, place a blackout slide in the chamber between them. This will ensure that your slides will not be getting ahead of or behind you. Finally, your very last 35mm slide should be a blackout slide. This will allow you to bring up the room lights without having to go over to the projector to turn it off.

The biggest potential problem you will face with a 35mm slide presentation is the type of screen you have. There are basically three types of front projection screens.

The canvas screen is the oldest type and is simply a square piece of canvas mounted on a tripod. Using a canvas screen is just about the same as using a wall to show your slides. You'll need to drop the room lights down to zero if you expect your audience to see the slides, which will turn you into a disembodied voice floating around the room. This situation usually doesn't worry speakers because they assume they'll be illuminated by the light on the lectern. That's fine, as long as the lectern light is working, which it generally isn't. So, here's something to make sure you bring with you (you can include it in your Disaster Bag, which we'll discuss in chapter six). Go to a discount store and buy one of those lights that attach to a picture frame (the ones that shine down on the picture and make it look more expensive than it really is). Attach the picture-frame light to your lectern or to the top of a table, so that it shines in your direction. Be careful to avoid shining the light too closely to the screen because you'll obliterate your visual.

The second kind of screen is called the beaded screen. This is the one your grandparents may have in their homes to show old home movies. It gets its name from the way it's made: it's a piece of canvas that has tiny glass beads all over the reflecting surface. This increases the amount of light reflected and improves the quality of the picture. If you are using a beaded screen, you can show your visuals in subdued light. This will allow your audience to continue to see you while you're showing the slides.

The third type of screen is called the lenticular screen. It looks very much like a canvas screen except that it has tiny lines of resolution running across its surface. This screen will also allow you to run your slides in subdued light.

Another type of screen is also used when showing slides and for vugraphs: the rear projection screen. Someone inside a small room behind the speaker controls the slides or vugraphs. Through a set of mirrors, the images of the visuals are projected through the screen for the audience to see. The major thing to be sure of with this type of screen is that you practice the presentation with the person who will be controlling the visuals.

I'll never forget watching a live broadcast of the Saturn fly-by. One of the project directors was giving a rear screen presentation using both slides and vugraphs. The slides featured pictures of Saturn and her moons and the vugraphs displayed telemetry from the spacecraft.

Everything was going fine until the speaker said, "Next slide please." The 35mm slide changed. He looked puzzled and said: "No, may I have the next *slide* please?" The 35mm slide changed again. He now looked irritated and said: "No, no, I need the next *slide please!*" Suddenly, from behind the screen you could here the muffled voice of the exasperated projectionist asking: "Do you mean the #%*&! *vugraph!?*" With an abashed look on his face, the speaker said: "Yeah, the vugraph."

I'm sure these shenanigans made a wonderful impression on the millions of taxpayers watching the program at the time. The point here is to practice with your projectionist.

Controlling and directing audience attention at a rear projection screen is done primarily with pointing technique. If you are right next to the screen, use the same pointing techniques we discussed for the vugraph. One of the more interesting pointing problems that crops up with 35mm slides happens when you use the pointing flashlight, or laser pointer. This device is used when you're speaking at a distance from the screen.

The pointing flashlight is usually an ordinary flashlight that has a stencil of an arrow over the light. When you turn it on, it appears as an arrow that you can use to point things out on the screen. Some of the newer models actually produce a beam of light that looks very much like a laser.

As simple as this device is, I'm continually amazed at how many presenters totally destroy their presentations with it. They will start their presentation with the flashlight off. Then, just before they are going to point something out on the screen, they will turn the flashlight on. An arrow will now appear on the ceiling. They will then point to something on the screen. Since they're nervous, the arrow will shake. After they have finished pointing, they'll bring the flashlight back in front of them. They will, of course, forget to turn the flashlight off. An arrow will now appear on some audience member's forehead.

If the presenter happens to be using one of the new laser beam flashlights, numerous members of the audience will be ducking their heads in terror trying to avoid permanent brain damage. In either case, few people are paying much attention to the presentation. So, let's take a moment to examine the proper way to use the pointing flashlight.

First, pretend that the flashlight is, in fact, a pistol. Tell the audience what you want them to look at. Turn and find it yourself. Point the flashlight at the item on the screen. Now turn the light on. Rotate your hand around the object you want them to see. When you want the audience to look back at you, turn the flashlight off and look at them.

Using 35mm slides can make a presentation look very professional. You can play with colors to separate concepts. You can make the background of the slide just about any color, and you can vary the size and color of the graphics to emphasize specific points. While 35mm slides can be more expensive than vugraphs, if you use a photographic process the cost is comparable.

FLIP CHARTS

Flip charts are also very commonly used in more informal presentations. A classic flip chart is actually a large pad of very cheap, very thin paper that you can write on with thick felt markers. There are two ways to conduct a flip chart presentation. You can prepare them in advance as you would a slide or vugraph, or you can use them to write on during your presentation.

If you are going to prepare the pages in advance, here are some hints. First of all, *leave the first two pages of the pad blank.* This will accomplish two things for you. Since the paper is thin, using only one page will allow your audience to see your first visual before it is time. Two pages of pad will make it impossible for them to sneak a peek. Second, it has always been my experience that if you use only one page per visual, the paper crinkles on the opposite side of the pad, making it very awkward to "flip" the chart. Using two pages makes it much easier and smoother. The only additional thing you'll have to do is tape the two pages together so that you can move through the presentation smoothly.

If you want to look very professional, here is a really helpful technique I've developed over the years. Go to your stationery store and buy some tab dividers. You've seen these dividers in schoolchildren's binders. They are made of clear plastic and are attached to gummed paper. Small pieces of card stock are included on which a subject can be written and then inserted into the clear plastic holder.

Take the gummed side of the tab divider and attach it to the two pages of the flip chart you want taped together. Now, since the first two pages are going to remain blank, leave the clear plastic holder empty. Your first real visual will be the second two pages. It might be an overview of the material you are going to cover. Gum those two pages together but put a piece of the card stock labeled "Overview" inside the clear plastic holder. Do the same thing for all the visuals you prepare for the presentation.

If you do what I just suggested, you'll not only you have something to grab when you need to change visuals, you'll also have a topical outline of your presentation mounted right next to you on the pages themselves. Furthermore, if someone asks you to go back to an earlier flip chart you won't have to go searching for it. All you will have to do is find the appropriate tab divider and flip back.

This simple procedure will make your flip chart presentations look very classy.

One more thing on preparing flip charts in advance. Your minimum letter size should be three inches. This will allow your audience to appreciate all your hard work.

Another way to conduct a flip chart presentation is to use the flip chart like a chalkboard. Again, tape every two pages of the pad together. You can use plain tape to do so since you are only looking for something to grab to turn the visuals as you go.

There are a few things you can do to ensure that your audience is getting your point. Let's take a few minutes and discuss them.

First, remember to make your letters and numbers large enough for everyone in your audience. The three-inch minimum should be applied here.

Second, try to give your audience "triple reinforcement" for the items you place up on the chart. For example, if I were giving a presentation on the levels of communication we discussed earlier in the book, I would do it like this:

"Now I'll discuss the first level of communication. It is called the **Intellectual Level of Communication.**" (I would billboard the words.)

I would then turn and write the word "Intellectual" on the flip chart and say "the **intellectual level of communication**" as I wrote it. I will also increase my volume since I will be turning away from the audience. This way, I am making sure everyone hears it the second time.

I would then put down my marker, turn back to the audience and say: "Now the **intellectual level of communication** refers to the language we use in our presentations."

You see, the audience got the information three different times. This makes sure that we are all talking about the same thing.

I did one more very important thing: I put the marker down. Don't forget to do that yourself. I once saw a vice president at a very large company forget to put a great big green marker down. He then proceeded to stick it in his ear with the top off. This was followed by his finger, which emerged green. He ended the presentation by placing the marker in the pocket of his whiter-than-white shirt. During the question-and-answer period the shirt grew an enormous green spot. It was fascinating to watch, but to this day I can't remember what he was talking about.

Another thing about writing on flip charts: don't be afraid to abbreviate your words. Remember, you are using the flip charts to reinforce points that you're making verbally. If it takes you a long time to write out your words you will slow the pace of the presentation and not gain anything for it. The general rule for flip charts is the same as for chalkboards:

Chalk a little, talk a little.

Abbreviating will also lessen the anxiety all of us feel about misspelling words. If you abbreviate, you don't have to spell them out.

Many presenters using flip charts will write themselves notes right on the charts, usually in very light pencil. This helps guarantee that they write the correct information on the flip chart during the actual presentation. In addition, they are avoiding misspelled words. It's a very effective technique and I recommend it.

Here's one more flip chart trick: prepare a portion of it in advance. For instance, you can put an organization chart on the flip chart before you give the presentation, leaving the individual boxes empty. During the presentation you can fill in each box as you come to it. Your audience will have a good general feel for the organizational structure and can become acquainted with the people as the presentation unfolds.

Generally, flip charts are used at more informal presentations. However, if they are done properly, they can be very effective at any presentation to a small audience.

CHALKBOARDS

Many of the tricks I just described for using flip charts can be used just as effectively with a chalkboard. There are a few differences, however.

First, always start a chalkboard presentation with a blank board. If you don't, your visual will be getting ahead of you. The only exception to this rule is if you have drawn something on the board that will only begin to have meaning to the audience when you have filled in the blanks. Our organization chart from the flip chart discussion is still OK here.

Second, whenever you're not writing on the board, put the chalk down. The chalk dust will almost always find its way to your clothing. Furthermore, don't lean up against the chalk tray that runs along the board. Doing so will cause snickers from the audience while you are turned away from them writing on the board, and may lead to paranoia as you try to figure out what the laughter is about.

Finally, when you are erasing a chalkboard, be sure to keep a banter going with the audience. Don't say anything substantive. You simply want to keep the audience's attention on you while they wait.

High-Tech Visual Aids

The future of visual aids, like everything else, is in computers. Computer-generated visual aids can be absolutely wonderful vehicles for communication. There are a number of "presentation software" packages on the market now that you should know about. Microsoft's *Powerpoint* is probably the best known, but there are also many others, including Aldus's *Persuasion* and *Harvard Graphics*. All of these programs will create beautiful presentations in full color and give you the ability to change data during the presentation. For example, say you are doing a financial presentation. You are trying to demonstrate different kinds of returns based on different scenarios. With a presentation program you would be able to enter numbers during the presentation and have the computer change the calculations to show different possible outcomes.

The new computer presentation programs also allow you to import "quick-time movies" that let you display videos, photographs, or animations during the presentations. All of this is really neat stuff. Everyone will be using these and even more advanced tools to one degree or another in the near future, so it's a good idea to know what's out there.

Treat these computer-generated visual aids as you would any others, but also keep in mind the following things:

1. You must know what you are doing with the computer. You don't want to be in the middle of a presentation, hit the wrong button, and watch your presentation evaporate into the ether. If you are worried about this have someone who knows computers run the program for you.

2. If you are going to present to a large group, you will need the ability to project the computer image onto a screen. This requires special equipment that can be expensive to buy, rent, or lease. The lightbulb alone for one of these projectors is around $600. So do a cost-benefit analysis.

3. Make sure you don't dazzle the audience with your special effects. I call this the *Jurassic Park* syndrome. The first time I saw that movie I was absolutely amazed by the special effects. Those dinosaurs were so incredibly real and scary. I just could not get over the fact that many of them were computer generated. It took a few more viewings to get beyond this and focus on the plot.

Your computer-aided presentations can create the same sort of problems. Your audience may be so enthralled by your computer tricks that they won't have a clue what you're talking about! Use them judiciously.

SAMPLES

Samples are anything you want your audience to examine, from a piece of rock to a circuit board. The main thing to remember here is:

#32 👉 **Don't give a sample out during your presentation.**

If you give a sample out during a presentation you might as well shut up and wait until the audience is through looking at it. Samples are like dogs and children in movies: they're notorious scene stealers. Your audience will be focusing their attention on either the sample or the current person examining it. In either case they are not paying any attention to you. You are now wasting time again.

Instead, start your presentation with the sample out of the audience's view. If you can't hide it somewhere, cover it with something. When you're ready to show it to the audience, hold it in your left hand at about your eye level. Then move your hand so that the sample is directly across from your ear. This way you can turn your head and point things out to the audience. Be careful when putting the sample in front of your body. If it's close to the color of your clothing it will disappear. That will do you absolutely no good.

When you're finished with the sample you should either hide it again or cover it back up. You can invite your audience to come up and examine the sample *after* your presentation.

MODELS

Models can be extremely useful in helping an audience get a true three-dimensional idea of your concept. If not handled properly, however, they can also steal your show. Always start your presentation with your model covered. Uncover it only when the time comes to show it to the audience.

I also strongly recommend that you "color code" your models. If you are pointing something out it will make it much easier for your audience to follow you if you can refer to a specific colored area. Remember, colors separate concepts.

When you have completed your discussion of the model, cover it. You can always invite your audience to come up and examine it themselves after the meeting.

HANDOUTS

It's not really a good idea to give out a handout during a presentation, for the simple reason that your audience will unquestionably read it. Inevitably, then, they will be reading a page other than the one you are currently discussing. By giving your handout to the audience during the presentation you hand control of the meeting over to them—not a good policy.

Understand that the purpose of a handout is exactly the opposite of the purpose of a visual aid. A handout *should* stand on its own. It is, in fact, a presentation. You are assuming that the person who gets the handout will understand its contents on her own. You will not be there to answer questions.

On occasion, however, you will have no choice but to give your audience the handout during the presentation. In that event, here are some tricks to help you maintain control.

First, prepare your handout as follows: use the same visuals in the handout that you will be using in the presentation. On a facing page, inside the handout, have a fully paragraphed discussion of the visual that matches what you are going to say in the presentation. Now, no matter where your audience looks, they will be seeing exactly the same thing. If you have prepared the visuals in this way, your audience will have plenty of room to make notes in the handout.

You can also prepare your handout as an agenda for your presentation. You can have a series of headings in the handout that match the subjects you will be discussing. You should leave two or three inches between the headings so that your listeners can make their own notes.

The only other problem you face is getting the audience on the same page as you. Here's how. Start your presentation with the handouts in front of each member of the audience. Let them take a minute to look through them. They're going to do it anyway, so you might as well make them think you planned it that way.

After a few moments, ask the audience to turn to page one. Then shut up and wait. After a few more moments, smile graciously and ask if everyone is on page one. (You can even worry them into it by asking if everyone *has* a page one.) Remain silent for a few more moments. This will clearly communicate that you are not going to continue until everybody is on page one. When you see that they are, proceed. Do the same thing for each succeeding page. You are now back in control of the meeting, where you belong.

 Visual aids can truly enhance a presentation, as long as they are kept in their place. Remember, they are supposed to work for you, not vice versa. Using your visual aids well should keep you in control!

CHAPTER 6

On Your Mark, Get Ready!

I'm going to make a deal with you. Do what I suggest in this chapter, and two things will happen. Your presentation will take you less time to put together. And your presentation will take a quantum leap in quality.

The key to the success of any presentation is, without a doubt, preparation. If you don't know what you're going to say at a presentation, it makes absolutely no difference how you say it. If you spend your time in front of an audience worrying about what your next point will be, you're wasting everybody's time and causing yourself a lot of grief.

To avoid this embarrassment, it's important to have a system for preparing for a presentation. Here's an eight-step approach that will take you from the time you receive the request to the moment you walk onto the platform.

THE ASSIGNMENT

Let's assume that it's 7:00 a.m. one Monday morning. You've gotten to work early because you have a tough week coming up and you want to get yourself organized. At 7:15 a.m. the phone rings. It's your boss. She compliments you for being at work so early. You remind the boss that you're one of her finest employees.

The boss now rewards you for being such a wonderful employee by inserting a verbal stiletto in your back. She says: "Hey, I've got a real *opportunity* for you." You know when she says something like that it means trouble. She continues: "I'm supposed to give a presentation next week to the local Rotary club. But, as you know, that is the week I take my son up to Camp Gitcheegoomie for the annual bake-off. So (now she turns the stiletto), I thought it would be *good for your development* for you to give this presentation for me. You can get the details from my secretary. Thank you for being such a fine employee." She hangs up.

You have just received step one of preparation for a presentation. It is called the assignment. It is also sometimes known as the shaft, the "Oh my God" phone call, and many other things. There are basically two ways to react to the assignment. The first is all too normal. It goes something like this: "That miserable so and so. Every time she has to give a presentation she bails out and makes me do it. I have a million other things to do. I'll put this thing together the best way I can and hopefully it will work out."

There's no need to respond that way. Instead, look upon this presentation as, in fact, an opportunity. It's an opportunity for a production. A production in which you are the star, the producer, the director, the writer, and the graphics person. In other words, this production will rise or fall on your performance. If you do a lousy job, you'll make yourself and your organization look bad. If you do a good job you'll make you, your boss, and your organization look good. It is in your best interest to do the best possible job you can because it will affect your career opportunities.

There are a series of questions that need to be asked at this stage of your preparation. I call them logistics questions. They are the basic questions of journalism: who, what, where, when, why, and how. Here are some examples of these important questions, which you should direct to the person in charge of the meeting you'll be addressing:

1. Who is the group?

2. What do they want to know?

3. Where are they going to meet?

4. When are they going to meet? What time?

5. Why are they going to meet?

6. How much time do I have for my presentation?

7. Where do I park? (This sounds like a dumb question. Believe me, it's not.)

8. How many people will be there?

9. What is the room like in terms of size and shape?

10. Who will provide the audio/visual equipment?

11. Are there any other speakers? If so, who are they?

This last question needs further comment. If you find out that there will be another person or persons speaking, it's imperative that you find out who they are. If they're *friendly* to your position, arrange to speak first. The reason is compelling. They may be friendly to your position, but they may be terrible presenters. If they are, they'll do one of two things to your audience. Either they'll anesthetize them or they'll outrage them. If they anesthetize the audience, you'll find yourself talking to a bunch of stiffs. If they outrage them, you'll find yourself talking to a bunch of hostiles unnecessarily. Neither case is to your advantage. You speak first and let the follow-up speakers rise to *your* level of competence.

The flip side of this is just as compelling. If the other speaker is a silver-tongued devil and wows the audience, you'll face the problem of following him. This can be disconcerting and adds a great deal of undue pressure.

If, however, you find that the other speaker is *unfriendly* to your position, then arrange to speak last. That way you can use a portion or, if necessary, all of your time to rebut what has been said previously. Remember, *last heard, first remembered.*

How do you arrange for the proper position? You simply create a reasonable doubt. If you want to speak first, tell the person running the meeting that you may have to leave early that day. This is not a lie. It's a *speculation.* There might be a supernova that day, or Atlantis might rise. If you want to appear last, tell the person you might be a little late that day. I have used this approach many times. I've rarely had a program chairperson turn me down.

Unfortunately, most speakers stop asking questions after the logistics questions. They figure they know who it is, where it is, when it is, perhaps even where they're supposed to park! But there's still much more to do.

AUDIENCE ANALYSIS

You're trying to put together a presentation that will prove compelling to a specific group of people. That will require step two of preparation for a presentation. It's called audience analysis. Audience analysis is taking the pulse of a group and finding out what makes them tick. To do this, you'll need to ask additional questions, not only of the person running the meeting but of anyone you know who is familiar with the group.

Audience analysis questions go as follows:

1. What is the purpose of the group? Why do they exist?

2. What does the group do?

3. What specific things has it done lately? (You might be able to refer to them in your presentation.)

4. Who is in the group? Are they business and professional people? Blue-collar workers? Students? Technically oriented?

5. What is the educational level of the group? (This will have a big impact on the sophistication of your material.)

6. What is the general age of the group? Are they senior citizens? Children or young adults?

7. What is the sex of the group? All male, all female, or mixed?

8. What is the political orientation of the audience?

9. What is the ethnic background? Do they speak English?

10. What is the income level of the group?

A neat book explaining the differences in perception between age groups is called The People Puzzle, *by Morris Massey. It will help you tailor your presentation to the values systems present in the audience.*

Now, why am I suggesting you ask all these nosy and irritating questions? Because I don't want you to walk into your next presentation with the *wrong* speech in your pocket. Furthermore, I don't want you to suffer from a condition I call Podo-cannibalism, also known as foot in mouth disease.

If you are giving your presentation to your internal management or to customers, you'll need to ask some additional questions:

1. Who is the decision maker in the room? What kind of person is he? Is he detail oriented or is he a "bottom liner"? Is he a technical professional or management oriented?

2. Who are the influencers in the room? Who are the people who are going to have a significant impact on the decision maker's decision? What kind of people are they? Are they detail oriented? Or are they "bottom liners"?

3. Who are my enemies in the room? Remember, reasonable people may reasonably disagree. You will want to find out why they disagree with you so you can "pull their fangs" before they use them.

4. Who are my friends in the room? Who can I count on for support during my presentation? I feel so strongly about having a friend in the room that, should you discover that you will have no friends present, *bring one with you.* Take my word for it, when you're talking to a bunch of sour-faced stiffs it sure is a relief to look to the back of the room and see a smiling face beaming out encouragement.

The importance of asking these questions can't be stressed enough. The information you obtain will be critical when you move on to step three, preparing the presentation.

Preparing the Presentation

In writing your presentation, try to do the following three things:

1. Tell the audience what *they* want to know. Essentially, you've been asked a question by the audience, through the person in charge. Answer it.

2. Tell the audience what *you* want them to know. In addition to the material the audience requested, give them some other positive information about yourself, your organization, or your subject.

3. Tell the audience something of future interest. In other words, try to mention something that will be happening in the future that might get you invited back. It's been my experience that exposure is the key to selling opportunities and upward mobility in an organization. Try to create those opportunities yourself.

In addition to preparing the presentation copy, you'll need to prepare your visual aids. The type of visuals you use will be determined by the information you obtained in steps one and two. I'll have a great deal more to say about visual aids in chapter seven. Just remember that this is the point when you actually put them together.

After you've prepared the copy and the visuals I suggest you do one more thing: plan your grooming. If you've decided that a particular article of clothing is appropriate for the presentation, make sure you have it ready. You don't want to discover on the day of the presentation that the clothes you were going to wear are in a ball in the back of the car on their way to the cleaners. Instead, make sure they are in your closet, cleaned and pressed.

So, up to this point, you've taken on the assignment; you know exactly what you are up against. You've analyzed the audience and know what makes them tick. Based on that information you have prepared your presentation, including your visuals, and planned your grooming.

Now you move on to one of the most important parts of preparing for a presentation. Step four is practice!

PRACTICE

You want to find out that your presentation has problems in practice, where it doesn't count. You want to find out that your thirty-minute presentation takes you two hours and forty-five minutes to deliver in practice, where it doesn't count. You want to find out that your visual aids are inaccurate, unreadable, and full of typos in practice, when you still have time to fix them.

Practice is critical to the success of any presentation. Yet, it's the one thing that most people neglect. We all tend to rationalize our way out of practice. We tell ourselves things like: "I don't have two hours a day to practice a presentation. I have a store to run here." Or: "I really should practice this presentation, I just don't feel like doing it at this moment." Or: "I still have plenty of time before the presentation, so I'll do it later."

All of us at one time or another cop out on practicing. So here's something I think you'll find useful:

#33 👉 **Frequency of practice is better than length of practice session.**

Most of us really don't have two hours a day to practice. But throughout our day we do have five- and ten-minute pockets of time. For instance, it's ten minutes to noon. At noon you're going to lunch with a friend. You can spend those ten minutes in several ways. You can keep doing what you're doing, call home, read the paper, or *practice the first five minutes of your presentation*. Later in the day you have another five- or ten-minute pocket. Practice the first five minutes again! Later on you have another five minutes. Practice the second five minutes of your presentation.

You can do *anything* for five or ten minutes. If you make practice a lengthy drudgery, you just won't do it. If you divide your practice time into manageable, bite-size chunks you'll find yourself practicing more often and building confidence for each five-minute segment.

"The will to succeed is important, but what's more important is the will to prepare."
—Bobby Knight

You should, however, have one full-blown run-through before you deliver the presentation for real. Your job in the run-through is to connect the five-minute segments. I think you'll be pleased if you use the question transitions we discussed earlier as the connectors. As we'll discuss later, however, this run-through should not be on the day of the presentation.

Whatever you do, make sure that you set aside *some* time for practice. It's much better to make a major mistake in practice than it is to do so in front of an audience

With practice you are likely to have a very successful presentation. Without it, the exact opposite result is just as likely.

THE DAY OF THE PRESENTATION

Now comes step five, the day of reckoning: the day of the presentation. On the day of the presentation, there are two things you should not do.

The first is practice. Don't practice your presentation *aloud* on the day of the presentation. I know you'll be thinking about it. Just don't run it through your vocal machinery.

The second thing is: don't discuss the contents of your presentation with anybody unless it is to clarify a point for yourself.

I make these suggestions for one reason. You don't want to find yourself in the middle of an important presentation, finish a statement, and have a little voice in the back of your mind ask you: did

I just say that *now* or did I say it this morning in practice? Or when I was talking to my boss this morning?

If that happens, your presentation will likely explode. You'll go through the following thought process: if I *did* just say it, I'm going to look stupid if I say the same thing again. If I *didn't* just say it, I have to say it because it's important. This process will be going on in front of your audience. It generally causes a puzzled expression to appear on your face which evolves into an look of utter confusion. This does not help your credibility or your self-confidence.

The point of all of this is:

#34 👉 **Say your presentation only once, with feeling, on the day of the presentation.**

Now, there are a number of things you should do on the day of the presentation. First, always arrive early, at least thirty minutes before you are scheduled to go on. Believe me, a room can be oppressive. Some rooms are hot, cluttered, and uncomfortable. They can make you very uneasy. By getting to the presentation early, you can acclimate yourself to the environment in which you'll be giving the presentation. I suggest that you walk around the room, check out the lectern, check out the microphone, sit down in the audience to see how you'll look from their perspective. In other words, make yourself at home. You'll find that this will make you feel much better about giving the presentation.

Second, be personally responsible for your own visual aids. I know that you can have other people set up your visuals. Just remember, however, that if the visuals are messed up during your presentation, it will be *you* who experiences the anxiety attack. Sure, you can chew everybody out after the presentation, but by then the proverbial boat has left the dock.

Just about everybody has heard of Murphy's Law. If you haven't, here it is: if anything can go wrong, it will. I happen to be a believer in Schwartz's Law: Murphy was an optimist.

Here are some of Mira's Corollaries:

- If you don't bring an extra lightbulb with you to a presentation, the one in the projector *automatically* burns out.

- If you don't bring an extension cord with you, the closest plug is *always* forty-five feet away.

- If you don't bring an adapter with you, your plug will be three pronged and the wall plug will only accept *two-pronged* plugs.

- If you don't bring a piece of chalk, an eraser, or a felt marker, there will be a chalk board and flip chart *missing* these instruments.

To avoid the time-consuming task, not to mention the embarrassment, of trying to scrounge up the appropriate visual aid equipment at the presentation, I strongly recommend that you pack a Disaster Bag. In your Disaster Bag I suggest that you include the following:

1. An extension cord.
2. An extra lightbulb for your projector.
3. A wall plug adapter.
4. Chalk, eraser, felt pen, and erasable felt pen.
5. An extra carousel for 35mm slide projectors.
6. If you travel abroad, an electric cycle transformer kit.

Disaster Bags have gotten me out of many difficult fixes. You'll find that most people running meetings will move heaven and earth to help a speaker in distress. However, that assistance will still take up valuable time, which you won't have to waste.

So, always arrive early, check out the environment, and make sure that your visual aids are set up properly. In other words, cover your own tail!

PHYSICAL PREPARATION

Step six is the physical preparation you have to do right before you go on. First, I strongly recommend that you visit the rest room before you deliver a presentation. I recommend you do so even if you don't feel a clear and present need. It has been my experience that if you didn't visit the rest room because you didn't have to go, you will experience a desperate need to do so about five minutes into your presentation. This can be very distracting to you and your audience. It will definitely contribute to the Rostrum Rumba (which we'll discuss in chapter seven). While you're in the rest room, check your grooming. Make sure that your buttons are buttoned, your tie is straight, your collar is neat, your accessories are straight, and your zipper is zipped.

If you are feeling nervous (and you will be if you're normal), try this breathing exercise. Take a slow, deep breath in through your nose. Hold it to a count of six and then let it out through your mouth. You don't have to make a big production out of this exercise. Just do it quietly to yourself. If possible, do this little exercise three times. Shoot for a maximum of six times. If you do it more than six times you are likely to either fall asleep or hyperventilate. Neither of these occurrences is conducive to a dynamic presentation. Done properly, the exercise will slow your heart rate, lower your blood pressure, and reduce the flow of adrenaline into your bloodstream. In other words, it will help you to relax.

Once you've relaxed yourself a bit, you need to redirect all that nervous energy into productive action. That is where step seven of preparation for a presentation will come in handy.

EMOTIONAL PREPARATION

You'll want to move to this step about one minute before you go on. Emotional preparation refers to how you feel about your audience. Earlier, I suggested that you would get from an audience exactly what you give them. If you want an audience to like you, you have to like them first and they need to see that you do. That will require a conscious psych job on your part. You will literally need to think: "This is a good group of people. They have taken time out of their schedules to come to my presentation and I appreciate it. They may not agree with everything I am going to say, but at least they are giving me an opportunity to say it. I am going to give them the best presentation of this material I possibly can, for *them.*"

This step is particularly useful when you are going to give an important presentation to a group of total strangers. It will change your impression of the audience from a group of judges to a group of people, just like you, who are interested in your subject. That is an important perception because it will reduce your anxiety and help you feel warm and friendly toward the audience.

Now you are literally ten seconds away from walking on. Time to move to the last step of preparation for a presentation.

PSYCHOLOGICAL PREPARATION

Step eight, psychological preparation, has to do with how you feel about *you.* It's where you put it all together. It's a conscious thought process and it goes like this:

"OK, I have taken this **assignment**, I know exactly what I'm up against. I have **analyzed** the **audience**, I know just what makes them tick. I have **prepared** my presentation based on that information. I have **practiced** it, and I know it works. I have gotten here **early. I look** good. I **feel** good. This is a **great bunch of people**. *You just watch my smoke!*"

You might notice a dovetail with something I mentioned early in the book—that you can control an audience's perception of you within the first three seconds of a presentation, and that you should be looking for good posture, a positive physical attitude, and appropriate grooming. The toughest part of a presentation is getting the thing going. The system I have just described will ensure that you walk into a room or onto a platform with a look of confidence, enthusiasm, and credibility. You will make that all-important first impression: a *positive* one.

How do I know this system works? Because I've violated every suggestion I have given you and I've paid for it every time. A short description of an experience of mine might be helpful here.

When I was working for a large electric utility company, I was asked to give a presentation to a group of freshmen and sophomores at a local high school. The subject was, of course, nuclear power. At the time I was a twenty-three-year-old hotshot. I was in a reasonably responsible position and I thought I was utterly brilliant.

When the request came in I took down the general information, put it in a tab file, and proceeded to forget about it. On the day of the presentation I opened up the tab file and noticed that I was supposed to give the presentation. I immediately hopped into my white utility car (I always felt like a narcotics cop in that car) and drove out to the high school. I got lost and arrived about ten minutes late.

I was greeted in the parking lot by a guy with a very long beard, wearing jeans, no socks, and sandals with rubber tire soles. I got out of my narc car, extended my hand, and apologized for being late. He looked at my hand and said: "I'm Brown, you're late, follow me." It was not your basic warm welcome.

I followed Mr. Brown into the building until we came to a large classroom with two sets of doors. I stopped at the first set and saw about two-hundred kids inside. I figured this was my audience. I started to enter when Brown turned around and said: "I told you to follow me!" I followed him.

When I entered the second set of doors, I immediately noticed three posters on the opposite wall. The first one said: "Kilowatt Warlord Go Home." The second had a skull and crossbones with the legend: "Nuclear Power Can Be Fun." The third was a picture of one of those movie mutants and the words: "The Children of the 1990s with Nuclear Power." (This was in the early seventies. Guess who they were talking about!)

I asked Mr. Brown if they were having a poster contest. He didn't even smile. Instead, he said: "Give your speech." I was beginning to think that Mr. Brown was monosyllabic. Now, I assumed that these kids didn't know their tails from first base about nuclear power. So, I decided to give them a fundamental presentation, a *very* fundamental presentation. I talked about the little *sleepy* atoms, Uranium 238, being attacked by the little *busy* atoms, Uranium 235, which made a little heat, which boiled a little water, which made a little steam, which turned a little turbine that turned a little generator that made electricity.

I have always been a bit nearsighted. I need my glasses to see things in the distance. I needed them then, too. But hotshots don't wear glasses. I completed my presentation and asked if there were any questions. Sitting about twenty feet away from me was an absolutely beautiful young woman. At least I *think* she was beautiful. Since I didn't have my glasses on I couldn't really tell. But through the haze of myopia she was gorgeous. I gave her my best smile and said: "Yes?" She smiled back and said:

"Mr. Mirror (I told her it was My-rah), could you tell me what would happen if there was a double-ended guillotine rupture of the primary core cooling system followed by a failure of the emergency core cooling system? Would that not cause a reactor excursion which could cause a meltdown of the fuel rods into the reactor vessel? Further, if there were a containment breach would there not be significant property loss and the potential for casualties?"

My face was suffering a massive meltdown. She had just asked me everything about nuclear safety in one question! I gave some sort of stupid answer which, in fact, was no answer at all. I was extremely embarrassed and not quite as hot a shot as when I had arrived.

I looked for help in the back of the room. I saw long blond hair and a pink blouse. I pointed in that direction and said: "The young lady in the back of the room." It was a *guy*. He got mad and everyone else thought it was hilarious, except me. I was now getting very red in the face.

Fortunately, I had chosen the class idiot. He asked: "Could you tell me the half-life of plotinomium?" I said: "What?" He was trying to say plutonium. He struggled with it a few more times and finally, in exasperation, said: "Mr. Brown, I can't *read* this one."

It turned out that Brown had written down all the questions. Not only that, for two weeks prior to this class he had invited every antinuclear power group in existence to speak to the students. I was to be the industry response.

Well, when I left, after a rather heated discussion with Mr. Brown about the educational process, I was depressed, angry, and humiliated. I went back to my office and called the division manager to let him know what had happened. When he answered the phone I asked if he had ever heard of a guy named Brown at this high school. He said: "Oh, that guy, don't *ever* go out there and speak to one of his classes!"

One lousy phone call. If I had called the division manager in advance, I would have known about Brown's agenda. With that knowledge I could have brought a group of highly capable, highly qualified technical professionals who were trained communicators. At least we could have given those kids both sides of the issue. But I didn't feel that I needed to do that. As a result, I did a disservice to those kids, my company, and the industry I had agreed to represent.

Ask the questions I have outlined for you in this chapter. Spend the time in preparation, and you will ensure yourself a successful, rewarding experience on the platform. Believe me, the alternative is not pleasant.

Here is a checklist for you to use when you are getting ready for your next presentation.

AUDIENCE ANALYSIS CHECKLIST

PART ONE: THE PLAYING FIELD

Name of organization: _____

Date of meeting: _____

Organization contact: _____

Phone: _____

Contact address: _____

_____

Time of meeting: _____

Meeting location: _____

Why are they having this meeting? _____

_____

What do they want to know *specifically*?

_____

Time of presentation:_____

Length of presentation: _____

How many in the audience?_____

Speaker provides A/V equipment? _____

Speaker provides screen? _____

Where do I park?_____

Do I need a parking pass? _____

What is the room like? (An auditorium? A stage? A dais? A conference room? A classroom? A gymnasium?)

_____

Room dimensions:

_____

Are there any other speakers?

_____

Who are they?

_____

What are they speaking about?

_____

Is this a panel discussion? A debate?

_____

Who speaks first? (If they are friendly, you speak first. If they are unfriendly, you speak last.)

_____

What else is happening at the meeting?

_____

Part Two: The Organization

1. What is the purpose of the organization?

_____

2. Why does the organization exist?

_____

3. What is it supposed to do?

_____

4. What is its history?

_____

5. What does its mission statement say?

_____

6. What has its membership been doing lately?

_____

7. Have they had a major success lately? (*You might want to mention it during your meeting.*)

_____

8. Have they had a major failure lately? (*You will want to avoid saying anything about this, so it is important to know.*)

_____

9. Does the organization have any policies or views about the subject of your meeting? If so, what are they?

_____

10. Has anyone else from your own organization ever spoken to them before? If so, how did it go?

_____

Part Three: The People

1. What is the educational background of the group? (Some high school, high school grads, some college, college degree?)

   _____

   Majors _____

   Graduate degrees _____

   Fields _____

2. What is the age range of the group? _____

3. What is the gender makeup of the group?
   (All male? All female? Mixed?) _____

   If mixed, how many of each? Male _____

                              Female _____

4. What is the ethnic background of the group?

   _____

5. What is the group's first language? _____

6. Do I need an interpreter? _____

7. Should my handouts be in *their* language? _____

8. What is the cultural background of the group? _____

   _____

9. What is the economic background of the group?

   _____

Part Four: The Key Players

1. Who is/are the decision maker(s) in the room?

   _____

2. Is the decision maker "bottom line" oriented or very detailed?

   _____

3. What decision am I after?

   _____

4. Who are my enemies in the room?

   _____

5. Why are they my enemies?

   _____

6. Who are my friends in the room?

   _____

7. How can my friends help me?

   _____

8. What are the "nightmare questions" I might have to answer?

   _____

   _____

   _____

Part Five: Sources of Information

1. The group contact.
2. The library.
3. News articles.
4. My friends.
5. Members of the group.
6. Organization materials.
7. Secretaries.
8. Anywhere else you can find it!

7

Adapting to Speaking Environments

In this chapter we'll discuss the environments in which you'll be giving your presentations. We'll start with some interesting theories about staging and setting up a room to your advantage. After that we'll cover stage presentations, dais presentations, and flat floor presentations. Along the way I'll show you some tricks on entrances, using lecterns, and using microphones, and then we'll discuss how to properly end a presentation.

STAGING

First, let's look at staging. As I explain these theories to you, it will be from the perspective of the *speaker*, not the audience. Keep this in mind, or the whole description will be confusing.

Imagine a speaker standing in front of an audience. He is on a vertical plane and his audience is on a horizontal plane. There is an imaginary line crossing his body at the waist. Everything *above* the line is *positive* and everything *below* it is *negative*.

I think most people understand the psychological relationship between up and down. We hear it all the time in our everyday conversation. People "rise to the occasion," teams are "up" for games, achievers "climb the ladder of success." Losers "fall to defeat," people "fall to disgrace," and we all sometimes feel "down." Most of us think of heaven being "up" and hell being "down."

You can use this information to your advantage in a number of ways. First, when you prepare your visual aids, place your points from top to bottom in descending order of importance. Your audience will unconsciously prioritize the information the way you want them to.

Second, use your gestures to show your audience which of two approaches to a problem you feel is more appropriate. You simply place your idea on a higher plane than the other approach by raising one hand higher than the other. If you watch the professionals you'll see them doing this all the time.

The next concept may be harder to swallow. Remember, this is from the perspective of the speaker, *not* the audience. Everything on the speaker's *right* is considered the *positive* side of the stage. Everything on the speaker's *left* is considered the *negative* side of the stage.

Left has always had a bad name. The Latin word for left is *sinistra*, which is the root for our word *sinister*. In the Middle Ages, a child born left-handed was often beheaded because it was thought to be possessed by the devil. Later, the concept of left as negative showed up on the crests of royal families. If a bar on the shield went from right to left, then everything was fine. However, if it went from left to right, it indicated a bastard son in the family. We've come to know this as the "bar sinister."

It even shows up in art. Next time you see a print of Leonardo da Vinci's *The Last Supper*, notice where Judas is sitting in relation to Christ. In Christian theology, Christ is said to sit at the right hand of God.

Today, you can see the concept carried through on television commercials. The product the sponsor wants you to remember is invariably on the right side of the screen, that is, the audience's left. This brings up an interesting question. If right and left are reversed for the audience, wouldn't the opposite of everything I've been saying be true? The simple answer is no, because an audience tends to identify with the presenter. What is right for the presenter is right for us. What is left for her is left for us.

> *There is a cultural implication to the way we prioritize left and right. You are reading this book from left to right. Therefore, your eyes are conditioned to scan material from left to right.*

In our civilization, left-handed people are still discriminated against. Think about your school days. How many left-handed desks do you recall? I will always remember my left-handed friends corkscrewing themselves into right-handed desks. Left-handed people are always the last to be seated in restaurants so they can get an end seat and avoid putting their elbow in someone's ear during a meal. Left-handed children are even discouraged from using their left hands. I've heard many stories from my left-handed students of having their left hands slapped or tied behind their backs by over-zealous right-handed teachers.

So, since there seems to be a response built into audiences about right and left, you can use it to your advantage. First, if you have the option, always place your lectern on the right or positive side of the stage. Second, always place your visuals on the left side of the stage in a subordinate position. The audience will naturally be compelled to keep their attention on you until you direct them to your visuals.

Now, with all of that as background, let's take you through a presentation from beginning to end, using all the tricks of the trade.

Walking Onstage

First, always *enter* a stage from the *negative* side. Remember, when you have been introduced, the audience will be scanning the stage from their left to right. By entering from your left you'll make it easier for them to find you.

Even if you do everything that I've told you up to now, you can still blow your presentation. Let's assume that you have prepared using the system we discussed earlier. You are psyching yourself up. You have your "Hook" firmly in mind. The master of ceremonies is reading the introduction you wrote. Your name is announced and you start out onstage with your left foot. You just blew it. By starting with your left foot, you are turning your body away from your audience. If you want to make a good first impression, your audience must see your full face. Therefore:

#35 **Always start your entrance with the foot closest to the direction you're moving.**

In this case you are moving to your right. Therefore, you should start with your right foot. If you have no choice but to move toward the left, you will start with your left foot. In both cases, the audience will be able to see your full face. There are still more potential pitfalls to look out for.

#36   Don't let your audience see your copy.

If your copy is more than one page long, and the audience glimpses it as you are walking onstage or getting ready to speak, it will terrify them. So, you'll need to hide the copy. Here's how:

1. Take all staples or paper clips off the copy.

2. Make sure the pages are clearly numbered and are in order.

3. Place the copy flat on the palm of your right hand (left hand if you are entering from the left).

4. Gently fold the copy with one hand, being careful not to put a crease in the paper.

5. Hold the copy firmly between your thumb and middle finger.

6. Turn your hand over and place the back of your hand on your right (or left) hip.

You can now walk on with the *Encyclopedia Britannica* safely hidden from the view of the audience. If the MC wants to shake hands, back him up behind the lectern, grab the copy with your free hand, and shake hands.

Now, as the MC walks away from you, watch him go. This will draw the audience's attention to him. This does two neat things for you. First, it prevents the MC from becoming a distraction to your presentation. If you start immediately and the MC walks funny or falls down, you'll have blown your Hook. Second, it will give you time to place your copy on the lectern without the audience noticing it.

When you place your copy on the lectern, slide page one next to page two. When you have finished page one, slide page two on top of it. You will do this throughout the presentation. At the end you'll simply have a reverse pile of pages to carry off. This technique won't distract the audience and will prevent paper rustling during the presentation.

The Lectern

The lectern is more than just a place to put your copy. It is the recognized position of authority in any room, and the person behind the lectern is the recognized leader.

If you suffer from the "Rostrum Clutch," the "Lectern Lean," or the "Rostrum Rumba," here are some tricks to avoid looking silly. For the "Rostrum Clutch" and the "Lectern Lean" I recommend that you approach the lectern, take your normal position, and then take one half step backward. This will do two things for you. First, you will be too far away to clutch. Second, if you attempt to lean, your subconscious will tell you that you are about to break your neck and stop the process.

If you have a tendency to "rumba," simply place your feet shoulder-width apart. This will stabilize your body and significantly reduce the urge to move around excessively.

A moderate amount of movement behind the lectern is perfectly acceptable. Just remember that you're moving in relation to a stationary object. This will magnify the motion in the eyes of the audience.

Finally, it is perfectly all right to rest your hands on the top of the lectern, on either side of your copy. This will leave them available for gestures when the urge hits, and will keep them safely out of the way when you're not using them. Just don't put any pressure on them—it only adds to the tension.

The Microphone

Microphones will be of great value to you if you know how to use them properly. First, don't rely on a microphone. Remember, a quiet voice amplified will put an audience to sleep just as fast as a quiet voice unamplified. As I mentioned back in chapter one, project your voice to the farthest object you can see and let the sound technician worry about adjusting amplification.

In your speaking career, you will run into a variety of microphones. Basically, they will fall into two categories: the unidirectional microphone and the multi- or omnidirectional microphone. Let's discuss them one at a time.

First, the unidirectional microphone. This microphone will accept sound only through the top. Therefore, it's very important to speak directly into the top of the mike. The best way to find out if you have a unidirectional microphone is to test it. I'll show you how to do that in a little while. If, for some reason, you don't have the opportunity to actually test the mike, you can determine its type by simply looking at it. If it has apertures, or little openings, running down the barrel, it's more than likely unidirectional.

The best way to use this type of microphone is to bend it toward you and point it about six or seven inches from your chin. This way you're enveloping the head of the microphone with the sound of your voice. Stabilize yourself so that you don't drift in and out of the range of the mike.

A much more common type of microphone is the multidirectional. The multidirectional microphone will accept sound from any position in the room. Therefore, your job is to be the loudest sound in that room. Otherwise, it may pick up other noises and interfere with your presentation.

Here is how to use a multidirectional microphone: bend it down and point it six or seven inches from your chin, just like the unidirectional mike. Now turn it and point it over your shoulder on the opposite side of the lectern. In other words, if the mike is on the left side of the lectern, point it over your right shoulder. If it happens to be on the right side of the lectern, point it over your left shoulder. This will give you a bit more flexibility in movement and won't interfere with your voice.

One problem with multidirectional microphones has to do with loudspeakers in close proximity to the presenter. Since these microphones pick up sound from any position in the room, proximity to a loudspeaker can cause *feedback*, that very loud, very upsetting squeal. The best way to avoid feedback is to test the mike. As we mentioned in chapter one, the best way to test a microphone is with your own voice. Simply count to ten. Be sure to use the same volume you'll be using during the presentation. If you use a very quiet voice to test the mike, someone is liable to turn up the volume, setting you up to blow out your audience when you start your presentation at full voice.

To avoid the feedback problem, move the mike around while you are testing it. If you hear an echo, or the beginning of a squeal, move the mike away until the sound stops. It may not end up in the optimum position for the presentation, but you'll avoid a terribly unsettling experience.

The multidirectional microphone can also come in the form of a lapel mike. These are very small and powerful, and sit on what looks like a tie clasp. This clasp generally causes all kinds of ridiculous problems for speakers. Many times the speaker will not be wearing his own tie clasp. In the interest of good grooming, he'll use the microphone to hold his tie in place. The microphone is now located directly over his upper abdomen. If he happens to be giving his presentation just before, or right after, lunch, the audience will not only hear his speech but will be treated to a symphony of gastric noises.

Instead, find your Adam's apple and attach the mike two inches below it. Be sure that it is pointed at your throat and is not touching material from your shirt, tie, blouse, or dress. This will prevent rasping noises when you move.

One important note. If you are wearing an expensive tie, blouse, or sweater, ask the program chairperson to provide you with a tie-tack lapel mike. The tie-clasp type will tear up delicate fabrics in nothing flat. The tie-tack mike pins on and won't ruin your outfit.

Something much more important than protecting your clothing is protecting your physical self. Remember, unless you are using a wireless microphone, you'll be attached to a cord. You must be very careful lest you find yourself in a crumpled heap on the stage floor. Here's how to avoid this serious problem. If you find out that you'll be using a lapel mike, make sure you wear clothing that includes a belt. Attach the mike as I described earlier. Run your hand down the cord. Lean to your side and pick it up with your thumb and index finger.

It now runs between these two fingers. Grab the cord with your free hand so that the two free sides make a loop. Take the loop and place it between the belt and the fabric of your clothing. The cord will now run down your leg, to the floor, and on to the amplifying system. It's attached to you and you're much less likely to trip over it. Furthermore, if you move too far forward, you'll feel the cord pull, letting you know that you have reached the end of your rope.

The last type of multidirectional microphone is called a lavaliere. It looks very much like a Tootsie Roll attached to a string tie. Simply put the string tie on and cinch it up so the mike is two inches below your Adam's apple.

Now that you know about entrances, lecterns, and microphones, it's time to learn how to end a presentation.

ENDING YOUR PRESENTATION

First and foremost, it's very important to *let your audience know that you have completed your presentation*. This sounds silly, but I can't tell you how many presentations I've seen where the speaker simply finished her last point, didn't tell us she was done, and walked in silence back to her seat. Everyone felt uncomfortable, especially the presenter.

As with most things, there are two schools of thought on ending a presentation. Some say you should end them verbally. Others think it should be done nonverbally. I happen to think that you should say "thank you" at the end of a presentation. Remember, an audience doesn't owe you a thing. They have given you their attention. They deserve a "thank you" for that. It's a nice, gracious ending to the talk.

Finish your last sentence, pause for one beat, and say "Thank you," or "Thank you for your attention," or any variation you like. If you wish, you can even add "Good luck" or "God bless" or any other nicety you come up with to end the presentation on a high note.

Now, if you don't feel comfortable saying anything at the end of your presentation, here's how you do it nonverbally. Finish your last line, take a half step backward, and nod your head forward. This is a signal to the audience that you have completed your presentation.

In either case, applause should follow reasonably soon. If it does, and it will, accept it! So many people end their presentations and scurry offstage before the applause really gets going. This can be very frustrating for the audience. Remember, they are applauding in appreciation of a job well done.

When accepting applause, simply smile and say "thank you" again. They won't hear you, but they'll be able to read your lips. Putting your hands up like a circus performer or clasping your hands and moving them side to side like a boxing champ are both considered in bad taste. Signaling for additional applause when it begins to die down is equally tacky.

When the applause does begin to die down, simply smile and exit, leaving the stage on the positive side. This will leave an excellent final impression.

MORE STAGE PRESENTATIONS

What I've been describing is a classic stage presentation where you enter from and exit to stage wings. There are other types of stage presentations that also deserve mention.

The first is entering from a position in the audience. To do this properly, you should arrange for a seat in the front row on the aisle closest to the side where you will enter. There's nothing sillier than watching a speaker climb over people in the audience to get up onstage. If you're in the front row you'll avoid significant embarrassment.

In addition to positioning yourself properly, you'll need to practice going up and down the stage steps. These steps can be tricky and dangerous. Stage steps are generally steeper and taller than ordinary steps. Therefore, if you're not careful, you can end up doing a swan dive into the middle of the stage. This is almost always unimpressive. The only time it isn't is when you can convince the audience that you did it on purpose to capture their attention.

My advice is to go up and down the steps a few times before the presentation, just to get used to them. This will avoid undue embarrassment, not to mention medical expenses.

If you want to give this sort of entrance a touch of professionalism, you can time your steps so that the foot closest to the direction in which you'll be moving across the stage is the one that hits the stage floor first. This allows for that all-important positive first impression.

The last type of stage presentation is one where you enter from a position already on the stage. For this one you'll need to put your copy in a manila folder on your lap. Whatever you do, don't leave your material on the lectern before your presentation. I did that once and the MC walked off with it.

A concern many people have about these kinds of presentations is what to do when they're not speaking. They're worried that the audience is watching their every move. This is simply not true. As long as you don't do anything outrageous the audience will pay little or no attention to you. They'll watch the speaker.

When the time comes for your introduction, simply smile pleasantly. When the MC has completed the introduction, rise from your chair and move toward the lectern, starting with the foot closest to the direction in which you are moving.

There is one potential pitfall to this type of entrance. If you're not careful, you can easily trip over one of the legs of your chair. To avoid this, I recommend quietly turning your chair toward the lectern while another speaker is up.

Stage presentations can be a great deal of fun. You get the feeling of a true performance. By avoiding the little problems we just discussed you can make them very positive experiences.

Dais Presentations

The dais presentation is generally associated with a meal. A dais is a raised platform that is usually two or three feet high and covered in carpet. Tables and chairs are set on top of the dais to allow a good view from the audience. In the center of the table is a tabletop lectern.

There are a number of things to watch for at these types of presentations. First, if it's a luncheon or dinner, there will probably be a cocktail hour beforehand. Big recommendation: don't drink any alcohol before a presentation! Alcohol slows the mental process and interferes with good articulation. In other words, it destroys presentations. Instead of liquor, stay with clear liquids like iced tea, club soda, or water.

The second thing you'll have to deal with is the meal itself. I've spoken at hundreds of luncheons and dinners. The meal generally consists of a green salad with a nondescript dressing followed by an entrée. The entrée is usually rubber chicken, cardboard roast beef, or canned yak. It is accompanied by a pile of little green ball bearings and some plaster of Paris topped with brown glue.

Recommendation: don't eat a big meal right before a presentation. If you do, you'll probably get sleepy and that will hurt your performance. Try to eat only high-protein foods. And stay away from dessert. The sugar in most desserts will thicken your saliva and make it difficult to speak.

After the meal, there may be a brief business meeting. Then comes your introduction by the program chairperson. By the way, make sure you bring an extra copy of your introduction to the meeting. Program chairpeople are famous for losing speakers' introductions.

This leads to the two great commandments of dais presentations. Commandment One:

Always know where your napkin is.

Many people put their napkins inside their belts to prevent them from falling off their laps. Be sure to remove yours before the presentation. You don't want to walk up to the lectern looking like you're wearing a loincloth. Commandment Two:

Always know that your napkin is, in fact, your napkin.

Occasionally napkins and tablecloths are the same color. I've seen speakers tuck the tablecloth into their pants instead of their napkin. This always makes for an exciting beginning to the presentation as dishes, glasses, silverware, and food go crashing onto the floor *and* the speaker.

One last suggestion: be sure to turn your chair toward the lectern. If you don't, you can easily jam one of the chair legs into the carpet when you try to get up. I once saw a senior vice president of a very large corporation throw himself off the back of the platform while attempting to get up. There was a great deal of stifled laughter as the poor VP emerged. He gave his speech that night with a broken wrist. He was so embarrassed that he didn't even notice.

FLAT FLOOR PRESENTATIONS

The flat floor presentation differs from other presentation environments in that you're on the same level as your audience. Flat floor presentations are done in conference rooms, classrooms, and auditoriums.

The main thing to consider in a flat floor presentation is the room arrangement. You want to maximize eye contact and be sure that the audience can see you. If you have a small group, up to fifteen people, try to set the tables up in a U shape, with you standing at the open end. This way you'll be able to see everyone in the audience and vice versa. This is a very typical conference room setup. It is also the best.

If you must give your presentation in a conference room with one large table, stand at one end: don't remain seated. Standing will give you a psychological advantage, and a much more dynamic and positive physical attitude.

If your audience is larger than fifteen but still reasonably small, say thirty people, then go to a semicircle. This will still allow for one-on-one eye contact and ensure your visibility. In audiences over thirty people, you'll need to set up in the classic "auditorium style." Ask whoever is responsible for the chair setup to "stagger" the rows. This means that the seats in row two will be placed *between* the seats in row one. If you set the room up this way, everyone will be able to see you. Also, make sure that your visuals are placed high enough for the audience to see them.

In any of these arrangements, if the sound system will allow it, feel free to walk around. You'll appear more energetic and the audience's perspective of you will continually change, keeping the attention on you.

Just remember that moving around *behind a lectern* can work against you.

Here's a neat trick you can use if you are behind a lectern. You can give the formal part of the presentation from behind the lectern. When you have completed it you can come out and ask if there are any questions. This does two things for you. First, you are verbally opening yourself up to the audience. By coming out from behind the lectern, you are removing a physical barrier. Further, you are signaling that this will be a less formal part of the presentation.

If you get jumped by a member of the audience, you can always go back behind the lectern and reestablish your position of authority. When things get positive again, you can come back out. Be careful, though, if you have an unfriendly group. I've seen some speakers end up looking like groundhogs in difficult situations. If you draw a tough audience, stay behind the lectern. This way you will have something to duck behind when the fruits and vegetables begin to fly.

 I think you can see that adapting to speaking environments can be easily accomplished with a little forethought and the application of basic common sense. The idea is to place yourself in the best possible position for a successful presentation. By watching out for the little pitfalls, you can ensure that success.

8

Fielding Questions

So far, we have discussed how to prepare and deliver a successful presentation, and how to control a presentation while you are speaking. In this chapter, we are going to talk about how to control a presentation while the *audience* is speaking—that is, during the question and answer session. In the immortal words of philosopher Yogi Berra, "It ain't over till it's over," and there's still work to do after you've finished delivering your presentation.

I've seen many presenters do a first-class job on their speech and then proceed to undo everything during a question and answer period. The ability to conduct an open, honest, and upbeat question and answer session can add tremendously to your credibility. With a little thought and some practice it can be done easily. I'm going to show you how to deal with the kinds of questions you're most likely to encounter. We'll start with the most common type.

INFORMATIONAL QUESTIONS AND ANSWERS

These are the most common kinds of questions because most audiences use the question and answer session to clarify points or uncover additional information. Since we quoted Yogi, let's use a baseball analogy. These are the straight fastballs. They come right down the middle of the plate. With practice you can almost always get a base hit. I've got a laundry list of pointers that you need to know to handle informational questions well. So here they come, fast and down the middle.

#37 Always choose your own questioners.

I'm sure this sounds silly, but it isn't. Occasionally, for whatever reason, the person running the meeting will want to pick the questioners from hands raised in the audience. Remember, you want to maintain control of the meeting. If you allow someone else to choose your questioners you relinquish control to that individual. That person may inadvertently or purposely lead you into a nest of vipers. You may find yourself getting nothing but murderous questions from which you can't escape because you aren't in control.

If you're told that someone else will choose the questioners after your presentation, tell your hosts, graciously, that you would prefer to do it yourself. If they persist, tell them with an easy smile that you get nervous when someone else chooses your questioners. If they still persist tell them that it is perfectly all right for them to do so as long as they know that you tend to throw up a lot when you get nervous. They'll usually reconsider their position.

#38 Choose your questioners from varying positions in the room.

Choosing your questioners from different areas of the room will do two important things. First, it will get you out of nests of vipers. If someone you have called on is asking you a nasty question and those around him or her are nodding in agreement, choose the next question from another part of the room. You can go back to the killers after they've had a chance to cool down.

Choosing from around the room also makes a good impression on your listeners. It makes them feel that you are being courteous, which you are, by giving everyone in the room a chance to ask a question. This can go a long way toward enhancing your credibility.

#39 When a person is asking a question, give her your full attention.

It's terribly important to pay full attention to your questioners. Many people have difficulty asking questions. They may not be very articulate. They may feel that they are asking stupid questions. They may simply have a hard time framing a question. Watch your questioner to see whether he is having trouble. If so, nod your head in encouragement to indicate that you understand what he is trying to ask you.

Also remember our discussion of nonverbal dialogues. The expression on a questioner's face can give you insight into the *intent* of the question. Many times the vocal inflection of a friendly question is the same as that of an unfriendly question. The facial expression will tell you the difference. If you aren't looking, you won't see it. If you don't see it, you're liable to walk into a buzz saw.

Too many speakers spend their question and answer sessions looking at the floor or ceiling while questions are being asked. This is discourteous to the questioner and often leads the speaker right into that buzz saw.

#40 ☞ If you don't understand a question, make the questioner repeat it.

Sometimes questioners get all tangled up in their own verbal underwear. This generally causes the speaker to negotiate the question. "Do you mean this...? No? Maybe you mean this...? Or perhaps what you're trying to say is this...?" These negotiations only add to the problem and further confuse the situation. The audience will either tune out or become irritated. So, don't negotiate with your questioners. If you don't understand what you've been asked, make *the questioner* repeat it. You'll find that the question will become shorter and more to the point.

If, on the second try, you still don't understand the question, ask the questioner for an *example* of what she is talking about. The questioner will usually either give you an example or draw an analogy that gets down to the kernel of information she is after.

Why should you do this? Because you want to answer questions that have been asked of you, not questions that you *think* have been asked of you. In the latter case you are dealing in irrelevancy at best. At worst you are opening up subject areas that you have no business talking about. Neither will aid your cause. You will either bore your audience or end up discussing things you are not prepared to discuss.

Always repeat or paraphrase the question to the entire audience.

There are lots of reasons for repeating the question so that the entire audience can hear it coming from you. Some of them are obvious, some of them aren't. The obvious reasons are:

1. **Some audience members might have missed the question.** This can be caused by sound problems or plain old mind drift. If you break right into the answer, you'll get a third of the way into it and someone will ask what the question was. Now you'll have to go back, repeat the question, and hope you answer it the second time the same way you did the first time.

2. **Repeating the question gives you a little extra time to think of an answer.** While you are repeating the question you can frame the answer. This will make your answers more complete and to the point.

Now let's talk about the less obvious reasons you should repeat a question before you answer it:

3. **You can paraphrase the question and subtly change its thrust.** When you've been asked a very specific and damaging question, it's especially important to be able to shift it over to one that is more general and less damaging.

Here's an example:

> **Question:** "How can you morally justify charging the prices you charge when you know there are people who need your product desperately but can't afford it?"

> **Repeat/Paraphrase:** "This gentleman would like to know how we arrive at the price we charge for our product."

By paraphrasing, I have asked essentially the same question but removed all the accusatory language. But be careful with this technique. If you aren't subtle enough, your questioner will tell you he didn't ask you that question and repeat the accusations even more pointedly. Practice this one with your family and friends. If you get caught paraphrasing, keep practicing until you don't. Then try it with a real audience.

4. **Repeating the question involves the entire audience.** Saying the question to the group as a whole will prevent you from having conversations with individuals in the

audience. These conversations can become very boring to the rest of the audience, and can easily degenerate into "mini-debates." It's tough for the speaker to win these mini-debates. Remember, it's a lot easier to sit in an audience and throw stones than it is to stand in front of an audience and catch them.

I think you can see why it's such a good idea to repeat the question. However, in small conference rooms it isn't necessary unless you want to paraphrase or you become aware of significant mind drift. Then you can use the repeat or paraphrase technique to wake everybody up.

#42   If you don't know the answer to a question, don't guess!

This is a *very* important suggestion. I've seen many people cause serious problems for themselves and their organizations by trying to answer questions when they know nothing about the subject. If you don't know the answer to a particular question, say this: "I'm sorry, I don't happen to know the answer to that question, but I'll be happy to *check into it* for you."

Now, isn't that a lot easier than trying to guess? Of course it is. You see, if you guess you may guess wrong. Then you and your organization will have to live with the consequences.

One strong warning: if you tell a member of your audience that you'll get him some information, please make sure that you follow through. If you don't, you'll erode your personal credibility and that of your organization. Also, take special note of the fact that I said "I will be happy to *check into it* for you" as opposed to "I'll be happy to *get it* for you." You don't want to be in a situation where you promised someone information only to find out later that it's sensitive material and not available.

#43   Limit your answers to a maximum of ten seconds.

When someone asks a question she is probably looking for a succinct, to-the-point answer. Unfortunately, most presenters give answers that begin at the dawn of creation and go on until the end of time. This drives audiences crazy and makes the presenter look foolish. In my experience, ten seconds is plenty of time to adequately answer a question. As an experiment, look at your watch and stay quiet for ten seconds. You will see it *feels* like a lot more time than it *sounds*.

That said, if you have a very complex subject you may need to expand your answer, although thirty to forty seconds should be the maximum. If you go much longer than this you are no longer answering a question—you are making another speech. Many questions can be answered very nicely in a few words. If the audience wants to know more, they'll ask!

#44 ☛ **When you've completed the answer to a question, don't say, "Does that answer your question?"**

If you look back at a questioner and ask "Does that answer your question?" the questioner will immediately begin to think that you don't think you did actually answer it. Implicit in that question is "Do you approve of my answer?" or "If you don't like that answer I have another one I can give you."

If you have answered the question to the best of your ability, then, with all due respect and affection, clam up!

Now that we've talked about the straight fastballs, let's turn to the killers.

ADVERSARIAL QUESTIONS

These questioning techniques can be used simply to keep you off balance or to tear your head off. You need to recognize the various disguises adversarial questions come in. I'll go through the techniques hostile questioners use, and I'll give you the countertechniques. With practice, you'll find that you're able to handle virtually any situation successfully.

THE SPEECHMAKER

You complete your presentation, ask for questions, and a person stands up in the back of the room and begins to talk, and talk, and talk. She's articulate, she's dynamic, and everything that is coming out of her mouth is extremely damaging to your position. Most presenters simply smile courteously and let the speechmaker tear their heads off. Don't do that! You are dealing with a professional, and she will not stop until you make her do so. Instead of becoming part of the audience, regain control by interrupting her. You don't have to be obnoxious or abrasive. All you have to do is interrupt her. As soon as you recognize the speechmaker smile graciously and say:

"Yes, I see that you have a lot on your mind back there, but do you have a specific question that I can answer for you?" If she continues, keep smiling and say this: "Yes, I understand that, but what is your question?"

If you begin to get a feel for what she is driving at, use the paraphrase. Say, "Oh yes, I think what you're really asking me here is _____." Then pose a question for yourself and answer it.

If she won't shut up then, say, "Well, I know that you have a great deal on your mind, but I think in the interest of time and in fairness to the rest of the audience, I had better give someone else a chance to ask a question." Then call on somebody else. This will shut her mouth instantly.

THE TRICKSTER

The trickster will make an impossibly confusing statement followed by a simple question. This is a tough one. The questioner says:

"Now, we all know that your organization has the administration in its back pocket, and that you're running a house of prostitution in your headquarters, and that you have been personally dealing in drugs for years, so I'd like to know how many members you currently have."

This little technique generally causes most speakers to enter "thrash-mode." The poor presenter hears all these terrible statements coming at him in waves, and goes into vapor lock. Like a drowning man, he sees a straw go by in the form of a simple question. He thinks: "Thank goodness, I know that one!" and answers the question without dealing with the statements. In so doing, not only has he answered the question, he has *endorsed the statements*.

You must deal with the statements. Here's how:

First of all, never repeat his language! If you repeat the language it will become quotable because it came out of your mouth. Instead, smile and say: "Sir, you have asked me an interesting question, but you have also made some statements that are completely untrue. However, the answer to your question is _____."

This technique is killing with a smile. It tells the audience that you have the questioner's number and will not let him get away with it. There are times when a presenter has to stand his ground. This is one of them.

THE DOUBLE BINDER, OR "HAVE YOU STOPPED BEATING YOUR WIFE?"

In this one the questioner asks the speaker if he is still trying to keep women and minorities out of his organization. The speaker becomes outraged and says "No!" thereby indicating that he used to behave that way.

The correct answer is as follows:

"Sir, I am amazed that you could make a statement like that. We have a very effective and long-standing policy to give any and all people the opportunity to join our organization and move up through its ranks. Therefore, your statement is both untrue and terribly unfair."

Note what I did here. I let the audience know that I had not really been asked a question. I was accused in a statement *disguised* as a question. Secondly, I used the statement as an opportunity to make a positive comment about my organization. In other words I "went to a commercial." I know that you have many positive things to say about yourself, your subject, and your organization. Grab every opportunity to say them, even in a tough question and answer period. Remember, always go to the commercial!

THE BALL OF WORMS

This technique consists of a series of three or four questions, all of which are asked at the same time, none of which are related. Speakers, in an attempt to be accommodating, end up negotiating with the questioner. They say: "I'll answer your third question first, your second question third, and your first question second." There is a pause and the speaker sheepishly asks what the third question was. This annoys audiences and makes speakers look like idiots.

The countermove to this technique is simple. Say to the questioner that she has given you a number of questions and ask her to ask them one at a time. The questioner probably won't remember all of the questions and will pick the most important one. You may now answer the question and move on to someone else.

Another technique is to mention to the questioner that she has asked a number of questions and then pick the one *you* like best— preferably one to which you happen to know the answer.

THE LEADING QUESTION

This is the most commonly used adversarial questioning technique. The questioner asks a series of what appear to be innocuous questions, all of which require one- or two-word answers. The questioner is leading the speaker to the *questioner's* conclusion.

There are two ways to deal with this type of question.

If you don't know where the questioner is taking you, ask him. Say something like: "You know, you seem to be asking me a series of questions that appear to be leading somewhere. Now, I suspect that we can save each other and our audience a great deal of time if you'll just tell me what you want me to say." This makes the questioner go to his "kill" question before he is ready to do so. You've just accomplished the verbal equivalent of "cutting him off at the pass."

If you know where he is going with the questions simply go to the paraphrase. Say: "I think what you are really asking me there is _____." You can now phrase the question your way and answer it in your own way.

The "What If" Question

This is a cousin to the leading question. It is different in that it is designed to get the speaker to speculate. Don't do it. Instead, tell the questioner that rather than talking about "*what if*" let's talk about "*what is*," and "what is" is as follows. Remember, reality is on your side, speculation is not. If you speculate you are on thin ice. It'll just be a matter of time before you find yourself in the drink.

The Interrupter

In this one a question is asked, you get a third of the way into the answer, and you are interrupted with another question. You get a third of the way into that one, and another question pops off. At this point you have zero information going out to your audience.

Remember to take one question at a time. If someone interrupts, graciously tell her that you'll be happy to answer her question after you have completed the answer to the *current* question. To fail to do this is to be terribly rude to the initial questioner and discourteous to the rest of the audience.

 So, there you have questions and answers—straight fastballs and all the trick pitches. With practice and some review of the principles I've outlined, you can easily become a .400 hitter—or better!

CHAPTER

Speaking through the Media

9

Why am I including a chapter on the media in a book about public speaking?

Because at some point, most of us are going to have some sort of encounter with the media. Fortunately, the enormous amount of television we watch has readied many of us for prime time. Each time a major national event takes place, I'm stunned to see just how relaxed we as a country are on camera. CNN takes its crew into a tiny bar in a tiny town in some enormous state with a tiny population, and the first person asked for his reaction to the latest crisis will answer, "Well, Bernard, I've long been concerned about the balance of power in that part of the world...."

Folks who would rather die than deliver two lines before a live audience feel perfectly comfortable sharing their innermost feelings with Tom, Dan, Peter, Diane, Geraldo, Ricki, and Oprah. We speak with them as with old friends. On countless occasions I've heard TV hosts say to their guests, "So no one in your family is aware that you're living this way?" to which the guest will answer, "No, I've never told anyone." Neither host nor guest will note how ironic it is to make that kind of comment before a viewing audience of millions, or how odd it is that we would rather speak on camera to a perfect stranger than phone up our parents with difficult news.

That said, conveying a professional message clearly on camera is significantly more difficult than spilling your guts. When you're telling a personal tale, the audience will forgive you if you ramble or use sloppy language—you're not expected to be finely tuned. The same is not true when you appear for business reasons. For an awful lot of people such an appearance is still an absolutely terrifying prospect. They imagine themselves in front of the camera, the target of an overzealous reporter, and their careers pass before their eyes.

These days, if you don't know how to play to a camera or use the media strategically, you'll be left in the dust. However, if you can present yourself well on video, the audience you can reach and the impact you can make get much, much bigger. Keep in mind the first law of dealing with the media:

Whoever controls the message, controls the game!

In my opinion, it's important to talk to the media. It's also important to develop relationships with reporters and editors. These relationships can become critical during difficult events. However, while I believe people have a responsibility to communicate with the media, I also believe they have the responsibility to choose the appropriate vehicle for that communication. I have some strong opinions on what kind of interviews you should do and shouldn't do. Unfortunately, that topic is lengthy enough for an additional book. Fortunately, unless you are working in public relations it's unlikely that you'll be asked to make such decisions.

So, this chapter will simply cover the basics of preparing for and executing a successful on-camera appearance.

Let's get started!

Before You Go on Camera

Whether you're appearing on the *Tonight Show* or taping an internal training video for your company, there are certain steps you should take to ensure that you make the best possible impression. As with any presentation, preparation is the key. I think you'll recognize many of these steps from earlier chapters, but with a twist here and there. With a few exceptions, the steps I'll describe would apply to any type of videotaping, from an interview-format news show to a teleconference.

THE ASSIGNMENT

You've been informed that you're going to represent your company on TV. It's time to ask some questions to find out what's expected of you. Direct these questions to the producer of the segment or program on which you're going to appear.

1. **Why have they asked me to appear?** This is a *very* important question. What is the theme of the segment or the program, and where do you fit in? We'll discuss later how to address the answer.

2. **How long will the segment be?** This is also a terribly important question. Will you have three or twenty minutes to get your message across? If you'll only have a couple of minutes, come up with a few short, meaty statements that will cover the basic gist. If you'll have longer, go into more depth

3. **Am I the only guest on the segment?** If not, who are the other guests? You can get a good sense of what the producers want in a segment once you know who else is appearing. Find out as much about the other guests as possible. If you're going to appear with someone notoriously difficult or verbose, ready yourself to handle him. Many interview-format programs feature three or four completely unrelated segments. Find out what the other segments are, and, if you can do so judiciously, make sure you're properly positioned.

This is more important than you might think. A friend of mine used to commentate makeover segments for a national women's magazine. Her presentations concerned how to use makeup and clothing to improve your appearance. They were light and upbeat; nothing controversial or difficult. As she waited to go on before one of these segments, she realized with horror that the guest appearing directly before her was the real-life mother of the child who inspired the movie *Mask*, the story of a little boy with a grossly disfiguring, and ultimately fatal, disease. This mother's tale was heartbreaking, and everyone in the studio audience (including my friend) was in tears by the time it was over. Imagine how ridiculous she felt discussing under-eye concealer and blush after such a moving interview.

While my friend may not have been able to change her position on the program, she might have been better prepared to deal with her segment had she asked in advance who the other guests were.

At this point you should also pull together some materials about you and your organization to help educate the producer, reporter, or host. They may include:

- A brief personal biography.

- A glossary of terms that are common to your work.

- Brochures on your organization.

- Some recent press releases.

- Black-and-white glossy photos of you or of any things of interest (products, buildings, manufacturing lines, etc.).

You can even pull together a videotape that features interesting footage of your industry or topic. This is known as a "b-roll" in the business. B-rolls are often used by TV stations when they are doing stories about you and similar organizations.

Take the time, within reason, to explain things. This information will be very useful to the producer or reporter, and will help you establish a positive relationship with her.

AUDIENCE ANALYSIS

Now it's time to analyze the audience you'll be reaching. Here are the questions to ask:

1. **What is the format of the show?** If you've never seen the program, do your best to watch it at least once before your appearance. If you live outside of the viewing area, ask a friend or associate to tape it and send it to you. If possible, avoid asking your contact on the show— producers are often seriously overworked, and unless you're in tremendous demand they'll drop you if they think you're going to add time to their workday.

   View the tape to get a sense of the tone of the show. Are they looking for upbeat, inspirational tales or digging for dirt? Will the other guests be newsmakers or at-home crafts experts? Tailor your comments accordingly. If they're looking for hard news and you deliver light anecdotes, you're going to appear shallow and insincere. Similarly, if they're looking to entertain and you refuse to lighten up, you're going to come off as a stiff.

2. **Who watches the program?** What is the average viewer's age, gender, educational level, and political orientation? Is the program on early in the morning for folks getting ready for work, or does it air in the middle of the afternoon for at-home parents or kids? Consider who the viewers are and why they tuned in.

3. **What is the knowledge level of the viewers?** Just as with a standard presentation, you must gear the level of your comments to the audience. Is it a general or special-interest program? Does the average viewer have any prior knowledge of the subject? Are you the main story, or are you appearing on a particular segment, like the science or financial report? Remember that your viewers will be more diverse and less familiar with your topic than any audience assembled in a room. Keep your comments simpler than you would for a live group.

4. **Who is going to interview you?** While the viewers are your larger audience, the host or reporter is your more immediate audience. If he doesn't find you interesting, neither will the viewers. What sort of guests does the host like and work well with? If the host enjoys kidding around with his guests, make sure you have some appropriate one-liners ready. If the host prefers to engage in serious and thoughtful discussions, don't be glib. Give him material he can work with.

   Also consider whether the host is likely to be sympathetic to your cause. If his name is Rush and you're a lobbyist for Greenpeace, you might want to spend a little extra time getting ready.

5. **Is the program live or taped?** Live programs must keep a tight watch on time and will cut you off mid-sentence if they have to. Taped programs are a little more flexible.

6. **Is there a studio audience?** A studio audience can have a big impact on the flow of a program. They generally make them much more raucous. Many of the audiences for the afternoon "parade of pinheads" are selected because of their interest in the subject being featured that day. Therefore, you are not being interviewed by an individual, you are being interviewed by a mob.

   The better hosts police their audiences reasonably well, but many allow them to run wild. Make sure you know in which situation you'll be operating.

The Logistics

Besides preparing for what you're going to talk about and who you're going to be talking to, you'll also have to handle plenty of logistics for a televised appearance. Here are the questions to ask your contact:

1. **Where is the show taped?** Programs frequently send cars for their guests, but if yours doesn't, make sure you know how to get to the studio and how long it will take to get there. Because they require large amounts of space, many studios are on the outskirts of major metropolitan areas and difficult to find. Now is also the time to ask where to park, how to enter the building, and whether you will need a pass. Understandably, security is often very tight at television studios. Make sure they've made the necessary arrangements for you.

   If the program is going to tape at your office, find out exactly when they plan to arrive. Make sure everyone in your office is aware that the press will be roaming around—you want to avoid unnecessary embarrassment or distraction.

2. **When is it going to be taped? What time should I arrive?** Producers frequently ask you to check in an hour or so before you're going to go on. They'll want to go over the segment, set up any visuals, and have your hair and makeup done. Be prompt: there are often several other guests on a show, and if you miss your slot they'll drop your visuals, skip your hair and makeup, or worse, simply cancel your appearance.

3. **Can I bring a friend or coworker?** Many people find they stay calmer before an appearance on camera if they have an associate with them. Taking along a friend or coworker is usually not a problem, but ask permission in advance. Frequently "green rooms," the place where you hang out before your appearance, are small and chaotic, and producers occasionally try to keep anyone unnecessary out.

4. **Should I prepare any visuals? Are the visuals needed in advance?** If you have photos or diagrams that illustrate your message, ask the producer if she'd like to use them. She'll sometimes ask to have visuals sent in advance so that she has time to review and shoot them. If you want to run an address or phone number onscreen, ask about it in advance also.

PREPARING YOUR INTERVIEW

Many people believe there's only limited preparation they can do for a television interview. After all, the reporter controls the segment, right?

Wrong. *You* control your appearance.

Keep in mind, however, that the number one role of the media is to uncover whatever is newsworthy—in other words, whatever is *exceptional*. The fact that most organizations and people run their affairs in a quiet and efficient manner is not exceptional. Therefore, anticipate that the host or reporter is going to ask you the difficult questions. If your company has just developed an incredible new vaccine, but a lawsuit was recently launched regarding one of your other products, be ready to discuss both.

Prepare to tell the host or reporter, and through him the audience, what he wants to know. That is easier to determine than you might imagine. You've already asked the producer what he's trying to achieve. You've watched the show in advance, and gotten a sense of the kind of questions—fluffy or hard-hitting—normally asked. You've found out who else is going to appear on your segment to determine whether they're looking for some controversy, and if so, what kind.

Now, you should make up a list of all possible questions you could be asked. If possible, ask friends or coworkers to help. Don't avoid the killer questions. Develop clear, concise answers for each, and, if necessary, run them by your management or lawyers. It might be a good idea to read chapter eight again for tips on fielding questions. Limit your answers to between three and twelve seconds. You are trying to develop snappy, interesting "sound bites."

You must also prepare to tell the audience what *you* want them to know. If the host or reporter doesn't ask you the question necessary to get your message across, you may have to work your message into an unrelated question. Occasionally hosts are poorly briefed, are going through a rough day, or simply have an agenda that differs from yours. Don't let their lousy or lax interviewing skills prevent you from giving a good interview. Develop some graceful segues.

On the other hand, be careful not to engage in shameless self-promotion. You can only get away with one foray into unrequested material before you begin to look disrespectful and rude.

PRACTICE

As soon as you find out you're going to be on television, start practicing speaking as fluidly as possible. Don't break up your sentences with huge pauses and unnecessary "uhs" or "ums." If the segment is live you'll be cut off, and if it's taped you'll be edited for time. This process can significantly change the substance of what you've said. Practice your message so that it flows nicely. If you can, try to leave an absolute minimum of space between your words. This makes your comments difficult to edit and gives you a better chance of getting your entire message on air.

THE DAY OF THE INTERVIEW

Many of the suggestions for preparing for a presentation I've given you earlier in the book apply to on-camera appearances as well. First, let's talk about grooming. As always, dress appropriately for the audience—don't forget the story of our friend on *Donahue!* But there's more to consider when you'll be in front of a camera. You must dress appropriately for the camera. The name of the game is simplicity.

Men should wear plain blue, gray, or charcoal suits or sport coats. Avoid houndstooth checks and tight, vivid patterns. They will vibrate on TV and distract the viewers. Also avoid light-colored trousers with dark jackets. The camera will distort the view and you will look like "legs almighty." Stick with blue, long-sleeved shirts. This will prevent too much contrast between you, the jacket, and the shirt. Cameras have difficulty with severe contrast. Finally, wear over-the-calf socks, shined shoes, and minimal jewelry. Don't wear more than a watch and one ring per hand. Leave earrings, nose rings, and large neck chains at home.

Women should wear tailored suits or dresses in subdued colors. Avoid pure white—it drives the camera people crazy. Pink, light blue, and other pastels are fine. Be careful with a bright red outfit. It can distract from your face, hands, and eyes. Again, go with minimal jewelry and accessories. Avoid large brooches and chains, and stay with small earrings, preferably not dangling ones. Don't wear more than one ring per hand. The idea is to have the audience focused on you, not on what you are wearing. Also, be aware of skirt length. You don't want to worry about how you're sitting when you've got something important to say.

Most studios have makeup artists. Whether you are male or female, *accept the makeup*. The purpose of television makeup is to make you look as good as possible on *television*. Their artists will apply minimal makeup to reduce shine on noses, chins, and receding hairlines. If they so choose, these artists can make you look great. Be nice to them, though—they can also make you look lousy.

Now it's almost time to go on. Do the breathing exercise outlined in chapter six if you're nervous. Prepare yourself emotionally: just as with a normal audience, you will get from a television audience exactly what you give them. Remember that the host or reporter has invited you to appear, and approach her as positively as possible.

At this point you'll most likely be asked to take your place for the interview. It's time to prepare yourself psychologically. Remind yourself that you're well prepared and looking great. You're going to get along famously with the host or reporter and do a strong interview. Have a seat, let the technicians adjust the microphone, and give the interviewer a big smile. You're ready to roll.

A side note: if you're doing the interview in your office, you should either stand or sit in an open chair. Don't lounge or hide yourself behind a desk.

ON THE AIR

Let's go over some tips for communicating your message on screen. Remember that television is a very intimate medium. It is essentially a one-on-one encounter with the home audience. The camera will pick up every nuance of expression. A slight smile can speak volumes. A small gesture can create a whole image. A fidgeting hand or a fleeting eye can betray anxiety.

It is important to imagine that you are talking to a friend. It is also important to fit your gestures to the size of the screen. If you make great big gestures they are likely to fall outside of the picture. Use the outline of your body as the boundaries for your gestures. Light up your eyes when speaking in front of the camera, and let your face communicate your enthusiasm. These are the things that will influence your viewers and leave them with a positive image of you.

Be aware that the camera is often on you for a few seconds before and after the interview. Stay dynamic and pleasant for as long as you're hooked to the mike. Look at the host during the entire interview. She is your audience. You should not address the viewing or studio audience unless your host directs your attention that way. Speaking directly to the audience appears presumptuous and arrogant when done by anyone who is not a celebrity.

Most important, stay cool. Remember, you've prepared for every question the interviewer might throw at you. Your objective is to communicate a clear, understandable message or theme to the folks at home. Don't get sucked into debates or arguments with the host or members of the studio audience. Understand that the host is a reporter simply doing what reporters do. Stay focused on helping the viewers understand your message. Keep your ego out of the interview. If you get mad, you're dead.

Please do not delude yourself that any reporter is going to support your position on any particular issue. A lot of people are furious when they grant an interview and the reporter doesn't advocate their position in the resulting story. Reporters are supposed to be in the business of reporting news in a *balanced* manner. That is, they are supposed to report all the angles on a story and should not support one point of view over another.

Lest you think I am some kind of naive moron, I understand that there is a great deal of unwarranted editorializing going on in what is supposed to be hard news. But, to some degree, that has always been true.

Remember the pressures a reporter must face learning about your industry in a very short time, then trying to communicate it in its simplest, most understandable and entertaining form to others. This occurs under extraordinary time pressure and competitive warfare. No wonder it's so often screwed up.

So, try to help the reporter. You don't have to give away the store. You don't have to spill your guts about everything you have ever known. You simply have to develop a message, stick with it, and do your best to help the reporter understand your point of view.

Occasionally, the worst will happen. You'll be asked a killer question you didn't anticipate and really can't answer. Do you say "no comment"? No way! Saying "no comment" is sort of like kissing a pig. It's embarrassing and it annoys the pig. When you say "no comment" to a reporter you immediately send a negative signal. It's like waving a red flag.

Here are some tips about what to say instead. If the issue you're asked about is in litigation, say:

"That is an interesting question. But as you know that issue is in litigation, and in fairness to everyone involved it would be inappropriate to discuss it right now."

If it is under investigation, say:

"We have a complete investigation under way and in fairness to the investigators it would be inappropriate to speculate about their findings."

If it is about something you can't discuss say:

"As you know, that is a proprietary issue and it would be wrong for me to discuss it at this time."

One last note: if you bring a blank videotape, the station will often give you a copy of the program. There is no better way to improve future appearances than by viewing past ones.

SATELLITE PROGRAMS

It's increasingly popular to conduct interviews from remote locations via satellite. The classic example of this is *Nightline*. Each guest is hooked up to a microphone with a hearing device stuck in his ear, and the guests speak directly to a camera, not a human being. This method is also commonly used in teleconferencing.

Playing directly to the camera is uncomfortable for some people, so here's how to do it. First, pretend that the camera is actually a face. It should be the face of someone you like, someone you admire, someone you sincerely want to understand your point of view. As you look at the camera, imagine the eyes of the face on either side of the lens. (Don't look directly into the lens or you'll look like you're trying to hypnotize the home audience.) Toward the bottom of the lens put the nose and just below it a nice friendly smile.

I know this sounds silly, but it works. When I'm training people to talk to cameras I will sometimes put a "happy face" around the lens. It serves the same purpose.

If you have to change views between two or more cameras, consider using the "eye bounce" technique. You do this by simply bouncing your eyes off the floor and then raising them to the new camera. This looks better than abruptly turning from one camera to another.

If you want to see how this works, just watch your local news. As the director changes the shots, little red "tally lights" brighten on the camera. This tells the anchorperson that the shot has changed. You will see her bounce her eyes off the desk and look up at the new camera.

RADIO INTERVIEWS

Radio talk shows have experienced a great resurgence in the United States. Just about every variety of program is floating around on the airwaves. The key to radio is remembering that the home audience can't see you. They can only hear your voice, the words you use, and the vocal personality you project.

A great friend and respected colleague of mine is Walter Cronkite. He once told me that when doing radio it is important for the audience to "hear the smile." In other words, you need to sound like a nice person. You need to communicate enthusiasm and commitment *vocally*. If you don't think about it, it is very easy to slide into a very flat, monotone sound.

There really are two kinds of radio programs.

THE FLAGSHIP RADIO STATION PROGRAM

Most areas have big radio stations. Many of them run talk radio shows that attract large call-in audiences. The nice thing about these kinds of programs is that your interviewer can concentrate on you. This allows you to have a conversation in which each of your vocal personalities comes through to the listeners.

However, it's very important to get a handle on the editorial position of the station and the interviewer as it relates to your subject. These stations employ people called "screeners." A screener's job is to weed out calls from drunks, breathers, and irrelevant callers. However, if they are so inclined, they can also screen out friendly calls. Sometimes hosts have screeners do this because it makes the show more interesting. Just be aware of the possibility before you do the show.

ONE-MAN-BAND RADIO STATIONS

These are by far the most common kind of stations. There are thousands of them around the country, and every one of them has an audience.

If you do a one-man-band radio station interview, understand that the interviewer may walk away from you in the middle of the interview. This is because he has a million other things to do. You see, he does everything at the station. In fact, he *is* the station.

If you find yourself in one of these situations, just imagine the friendly face again. This time it will be looking back at you from the floor or the table where you are seated. While the interviewer is away, just tell your story to the friendly face. This way your vocal personality will be carried through to the guy listening to the show.

I think one-man-band radio stations are great fun and a wonderful way to develop your skill.

 The media continue to have a tremendous impact on our society. With the new technologies of communication and the advent of the information highway, your ability to present yourself on camera will become more and more critical. Master these skills—they will pay big dividends.

CHAPTER 10

Some Final Thoughts

I mentioned at the beginning of our time together that it's always great to watch people communicate when they're relaxed and natural. What I've tried to do in this book is to help you be more relaxed and natural in all kinds of public speaking environments.

To be honest, I think people make too much about getting up in front of a group and making some sort of presentation. Maybe it comes from our school days when we had to get up in front of the class and read a poem or a paper we had written or do some incomprehensible math problem. Maybe it's just that most of us would prefer to be left alone to do our work and not have to tell everybody about it. Maybe it goes back to our adolescent years when we were so afraid of making a fool out of ourselves in front of our peers. Whatever the cause, it's important to move beyond this anxiety in order to be successful.

More than just helping you feel comfortable, I've also tried to help you develop a healthy attitude toward public speaking. If there is one thing to remember from this book it is this: when you give a speech, when you give a presentation, you are giving a *gift*.

It is not a test! It was never meant to be a test. The test of your competence is in the preparation of your presentation. That is why so much of this book is dedicated to helping you prepare in an effective and timely way.

Be a student of presenters. You'll see many different and effective styles. You'll see those presenters who are able to flow through a presentation with little effort. These are the naturals. They're wonderful to watch because of the energy they exude and the fun they're having as they speak. You'll also see speakers who will fall all over themselves, not because they can't communicate, but because they just didn't take the time to prepare.

But you'll also see many presenters who will draw your respect. These are the speakers who have obviously spent time trying to prepare a presentation that is worthwhile and meaningful to you, their audience. When you watch one of these speakers, you'll realize that he is a little nervous at the beginning of his presentation. You might even feel a little empathetic nervousness as he begins.

But as the presentation unfolds you hear the speaker's voice strengthen, you hear the volume rise, you hear the subtle modulation as he moves through the textures of the presentation. As the speaker continues you see the beginnings of a quick gesture. Then more frequent and graceful motions begin as he forgets about the fact that he is giving a presentation and loses himself in the joy of helping you understand the message.

This type of speaker's visual aids are not made up of tiny words and unreadable, tangled graphics. Neither are they so obvious as to be unnecessary. Each one has a message that enhances the points that the speaker is making. Each visual adds to our understanding and complements and illuminates the message. This speaker does not rely on her visuals to make a point. We in the audience know that should the projector light burn out or a power failure occur the speaker could easily tell us her story without a single visual aid— the speaker herself would become the visual aid.

This type of speaker always treats her audience with courtesy and respect. In reality, the speaker and the audience are trading gifts. We give the speaker the gift of our time and the speaker gives us the gift of her knowledge. This is truly a big occasion—mutual respect is totally appropriate!

If the speaker is challenged from the audience, he will listen with respect because it is understood that everyone is entitled to an opinion and that it is from discussion that truth is discovered. He shows no anger or abrasiveness, even when he feels them from a member of the audience. This speaker knows that audiences are not stupid and that they have the same sense of fairness and proper behavior that he has.

Most important, this speaker has confidence, but not an overinflated ego. She understands that this presentation is given to be of value to the audience, not as an exercise in conceit. She understands that no one has all the answers even to the most simple problems and that her point of view is meant to add to knowledge, not force a particular course of action. Instead, this speaker will think the issue through, explain alternatives, and honestly and forthrightly tell the group why she believes a particular solution is in the best interest of all involved.

 I know all of this may sound pretty idealistic, but I also know that it's something we can all strive to achieve. There's a lot you can do to bring it about. Read this book often. Work on your skills one at a time. Actively seek opportunities to speak. Start a speaking club at work or school. Believe me, becoming a better public speaker will pay off for you. I know what it feels like to connect with an audience and be carried away by the joy of the communication. I have even had the extraordinary satisfaction of helping others achieve that for themselves. It is my most sincere wish that you, too, will experience these wonderful moments.

Diaphragmatic Breathing Exercises

1. TO DEVELOP THE DIAPHRAGM AND OTHER RESPIRATORY MUSCLES:

Stand with feet eighteen inches apart, hands on hips, mouth wide open. Inhale, pushing out abdomen. This will stretch diaphragm and other respiratory muscles. Exhale, pulling in abdomen to contract diaphragm and muscles. Do twelve repetitions six times per day.

Note:

- Your chest should only move below your sternum, where your ribs meet in the center of your body.

- Inhale as deeply as you can, stretching the diaphragm, then exhale, pulling in with the muscles as if you want to bounce them off your backbone. (You must think of this as a physical exercise and not just a panting session.)

- Keep the mouth and throat wide open while inhaling and exhaling. Allow a free flow of air.

- If you get dizzy, stop. Wait until dizziness subsides and continue with the exercise.
- This exercise should be done standing, but can be accomplished sitting, walking, or reclining.

2. TO DEVELOP THE UPPER RESPIRATORY MUSCLES (INTERIOR INTERCOSTALS):

Stand with feet eighteen inches apart, hands at sides, palms forward. Rise up on toes, stretch hands toward upper corners of room while inhaling deeply. Come down off toes and bring hands back to sides while exhaling. Do twelve repetitions three times per day.

Note: you may notice a tingling sensation beneath the center of your rib cage. This is quite normal.

3. TO DEVELOP THE LOWER RESPIRATORY MUSCLES (EXTERIOR INTERCOSTALS):

Stand with feet tightly together. Bend forward toward floor as far as is comfortable, clasping hands. Turn to left as far as possible, inhaling deeply through mouth. Turn back to forward position and exhale fully. Turn to right while inhaling, then forward and exhale. Do six repetitions on each side, three times per day.

Note: you will feel a stretching sensation in your sides during and immediately after you have completed this exercise.

Pointer Checklist

#1: Find the farthest object in the room and project your voice to that object.

#2: A quiet voice amplified will put an audience to sleep just as fast as a quiet voice unamplified will.

#3: Focus on what you have to say—not on the fact that you are saying it!

#4: Using conversational language is the best way to assure common understanding among the members of your audience.

#5: If you use a piece of jargon, follow it with a comma and a phrase that explains it.

#6: The first time you use an acronym, give its full name.

#7: Be very careful about the use of slang in your presentations. Be sure everyone will understand what you mean.

#8: Be sure to pronounce words correctly. If you are not sure about a pronunciation, look the word up in the dictionary.

#9: Concentrate on clear, crisp articulation throughout your presentation.

#10: You will *get* from an audience exactly what you *give* them.

#11: An audience owes you nothing!

#12: It is not just *what* you say that counts—it's *how you say it*. If you mean what you say, say it like you mean it.

#13: A presentation is a communication among a group of individuals, one of whom is speaking *aloud* at any given time.

#14: Always give your audience eye contact because:
1. It involves your audience.
2. It keeps you aware of their reactions to what you say.
3. It helps you identify friends and predators.

#15: When reading nonverbal information look for "clusters" of information, *not* individual signals.

#16: The expression on your face must match the meaning of the words you are using.

#17: Use your face to communicate what you are honestly feeling and as a part of your personal trademark.

#18: Your eyes communicate commitment and belief. Make sure you let your audience see them.

#19: An audience's initial impression of a speaker is made within the first three seconds of the time the audience sees him.

#20: Your grooming should be reflective of your audience and should never be extreme.

#21: If you use your hands in normal conversation, use them in your presentation.

#22: The bigger the audience, the bigger your gestures, facial expressions, and body movements must be.

#23: The single best way to have a successful presentation is to prepare properly.

#24: If you are reasonably sure that a difficult subject is going to come up during your presentation, raise it yourself in the form of a question transition.

#25: No more than five lines to any one visual. No more than five words to any one line.

#26: Stay with one major subject per visual.

#27: If you don't want to talk about something, don't put it on a visual.

#28: Always stay close to your visual aid.

#29: A visual aid should never get ahead of you.

#30: A visual aid should never get behind you.

#31: If you want the audience to look at the screen, you look at it. If you want the audience to look at you, you look at them.

#32: Don't give a sample out during your presentation.

#33: Frequency of practice is better than length of practice session.

#34: Say your presentation only once, with feeling, on the day of the presentation.

#35: Always start your entrance with the foot closest to the direction you're moving.

#36: Don't let your audience see your copy.

#37: Always choose your own questioners.

#38: Choose your questioners from varying positions in the room.

#39: When a person is asking a question, give her your full attention.

#40: If you don't understand a question, make the questioner repeat it.

#41: Always repeat or paraphrase the question to the entire audience.

#42: If you don't know the answer to a question, don't guess!

#43: Limit your answers to a maximum of ten seconds.

#44: When you've completed the answer to a question, don't say, "Does that answer your question?"